PHOTOGRAPHY - TEXT - ART DIRECTION
David Douglas Duncan

PRINTING
Imprimerie Centrale Lausanne

COLOR ENGRAVING
Clichés Actual, Bienne ; Schwitter, Basel ;
Steiner, Basel ; Imprimeries Réunies, Lausanne

BINDING
Maurice Busenhart, Lausanne ; Mayer & Soutter, Lausanne

PRODUCED BY
David Douglas Duncan - Ami Guichard, Edita, Lausanne

PRINTED IN SWITZERLAND

Picasso's
Picassos

PRODUCTION
E D I T A

Picasso's Picassos

by

David Douglas Duncan

Publishers   Harper & Brothers   New York

This book is protected by copyright under the terms of the International Copyright Union.
Permission to use any portion of the text or photographs must be obtained from the publisher. All rights reserved.
Library of Congress catalogue card number: 61-10205.

The Treasures of La Californie

To
The Maestro

No painter of this century's Midas-touched art world has seen more of his colors and canvas change to gold than Pablo Picasso: no painter of any century rose farther above misery and starvation to enjoy the frontierless freedom of universal acclaim. Today, although he is almost regally disdainful of all such homage, just as he was of derision in his youth, Picasso must get some satisfaction from the fact that there has never before been a man who lived to see the work of his hands win richer rewards. And yet, still shunning the clamor of controversy and persistent collectors, only he, among all artists, is known to have concealed hundreds of great canvases painted throughout his lifetime just because he cherished them himself, as his own offspring, and planned that they remain forever together.

As the years, then decades, carried Picasso deeper into this century, recurrent, always vague rumors hinted of buried masterpieces unlike anything known. Only a tight knot of his closest friends, probably no more than three, ever saw any of the pictures but they, like the Maestro, never spoke of the hoard. Noncommittal shrugs met all queries. Picasso's Picassos were a bonanza of art enshrouded in mystery. It was thought certain to exist, though just where no one could precisely say . . . no one but Picasso, who lived in isolation nearly as impenetrable as that surrounding the cache itself. To discover the hidden paintings might be as rewarding as piercing the sealed vault guarding Tutankhamon's treasury in the Valley of Kings along the Upper Nile. To photograph Picasso's Picassos became a dream of dreams.

Five years ago, in the spring of '56, while switching from one assignment on the Russian frontier of Afghanistan to another with the Berber tribes in the High Atlas Mountains of Morocco, my work as a foreign correspondent took me through Cannes, on the French Riviera where Picasso makes his home. Within twenty-four hours a wave of luck had swept me up to the artist's villa gate, which opened, to his front door, which opened, to his bedroom door, which opened—to reveal the Maestro himself, stark naked, submerged in his bathtub waving me a cheery welcome. My photography with him began that day, at that moment, in fact—as did an immediate and extraordinarily deep friendship. This first sudsy encounter heralded my return to the villa, *La Californie*, a few months later when I was to start spending more time in Picasso's home than any other in which I have lived, including my own, for more than twenty-five years. It also resulted in a book, *The Private World of Pablo Picasso*, introducing the outside world to the Maestro's self-contained universe which he, incredibly hard working yet often carefree, shares with his wife, Jacqueline. In the following years, although my cameras took me to many faraway lands, *La Californie*'s gates always remained open whenever I returned to Cannes.

One noon, while walking from his second floor sitting room around through the bathroom, headed downstairs for lunch (he always follows precisely the same route from one floor to another in the villa, and the same combination of streets while being driven through Cannes—rather surprising, when one reflects on his unconventional, unpredictable, approach to art) Picasso took me by the arm and asked whether I might not like to look into an adjacent room before we ate. I had stopped at the villa enroute to Paris, then New York where I was deeply involved in publishing a book on the crown jewels of Tzarist Russia. Many of its deadlines were on top of me, as I explained to the Maestro. I added that I intended driving through the night to catch my plane, so had very little extra time. Picasso still gripped my arm. I followed him when he unlocked the darkened room—and walked into the center of countless, precision-stacked canvases. I stood, quite literally, shoulder deep among Picasso's Picassos, the greatest unrecorded treasure in modern art. For three years I had passed this door never guessing what was inside.

Throwing open the room's shuttered windows, Picasso turned to me with a small boy's grin as the sunlight poured in upon the paintings. For the next three hours he, Jacqueline, and I took turns spinning around canvas after canvas that had been racked face to the wall, while the other two sat in ancient chairs dragged from the sitting room next door. Paintings ranging from nine feet wide to a few inches square lined the walls, covered the floor, were stacked on tables and disconnected radiators. I estimated that there were nearly two hundred pictures in this one room (I was wrong: there were more than three hundred) which were unknown. I remember that I said almost nothing. But Picasso nodded and welcomed each revealed painting as if he were witnessing the return home of a long wandering child. Apparently many of the canvases had been locked for years in strong-rooms of the Bank of France. Others had been silently disappearing under the aeolian dust of his long-closed Paris studios. Only during recent years, after making his home permanently on the Riviera, had Picasso started quietly gathering them all together for the first time.

For three hours, in that sunstreaked room, I saw Pablo Picasso's life laid bare. There were pictures painted when Spain, his birthplace, was convulsed by civil war—and the canvases mourned her dead; pictures painted when he was in love, and the colors sang songs of his own invention, later to be familiar in many distant lands; paintings when he was heartbroken and desolate (" The worst time of my life! ") and his brush spared nothing; portraits of children where their world and his were one; paintings so complex in concept and execution that they may well have been created generations, possibly even centuries, before the day when they would be fully understood; and pictures such as the profile of his daughter in her ski cap looking down at winter's first snow, which, when known, will rank second to none as the work of an acutely perceptive classical genius using only canvas and colors to tell his story. There were paintings dating back through the twentieth century, through each artistic adventure Picasso experienced during his fabulous life's journey . . . all unknown. There was a deeply religious *Flight to Egypt*, painted when he was a boy of fourteen, in which the Christ Child reaches exploringly for the beard of Joseph while the Holy Family wearily rests beside the road (" The influence of my father "—Picasso's first art teacher); and a scene of a bride being abandoned at the altar by her recently beloved, who suffers a last minute change of heart and bolts for the door.

There were collages, Cubist works and African, and a series of still lifes in which each flower's petals, each piece of fruit, every cup and saucer and knife was reality transplanted in paint. Other canvases revealed whole races of creatures never seen on Earth. Finally, with many stacks of paintings still untouched, Picasso called a halt, closed the windows and shutters—returning the canvases to their protective gloom—and we headed downstairs for lunch, which had been kept waiting. On the villa's spiral staircase I called down (he was whistling a Mexican army marching song with Jacqueline on his arm) that the unknown paintings would make a tremendous picture story. The Maestro, without turning, or stopping, scarcely missing a note in his song, raised his right index finger—the bandmaster demanding flawless response to his baton—and called back, " Fine! But only in color. " During lunch, when I got excited thinking of the picture possibilities in what I had just seen and stopped eating, he snorted with indignation. " Clear your plate—in Catalonia we have a special word for anyone who wastes food! " Jacqueline kept smiling as though over a wondrous unshared secret. Then Picasso explained: I had seen just *one* room of unknown paintings; there was still another in *La Californie*, and two more in his ancient *Château de Vauvenargues*, near Aix-en-Provence. His only reply to my wondering how many there were altogether, was " All you want. "

Several weeks later in New York, while discussing the Maestro's offer with friends in the magazine and book publishing world, I suddenly realized that I was talking of making a deluxe edition of Picasso's unknown paintings without his permission. On the staircase of *La Californie* I had only suggested shooting a *cuento*, story, around his hidden works, not a *libro*, book. In Spanish, our mutual language, there was no possibility of confusion. I got on the overseas telephone and explained my dilemma. Picasso's reply was typical. " Do both! " I could practically see the half-smile and shrug—as though what he was offering me was an everyday gesture. Then he asked when I would return to *La Californie* to start work—and to accompany him and Jacqueline to the weekend bullfights. As casually as that first morning when he had greeted me from his bathtub, he had just given permission for the most exciting and valuable book in modern art today.

Now, a year has passed. Over five hundred of Picasso's Picassos have been photographed in full color—the entire contents of *La Californie*. The majority of them are totally unknown. Many are canvases not only unseen and never recorded, but unlike any other Picassos in existence. Some were painted around the turn of the century and are the very roots of Cubism, which freed art of later generations from its past. During the mid-'30s very few canvases came from Picasso's studio. Friends had variously reported him ill, burdened with endless emotional crises in his home, writing poetry for his own amusement, painting a scattering of portraits of his companions of that epoch, and feverishly attacking the enormous mural *Guernica*, his later world famous, complacency-shattering protest against German bombing of a Spanish town on market day . . . a gigantic canvas, finished in one month. Apart from this—which for Picasso was almost inertia itself—nothing more was known of his activities. He was painting! Painting with perhaps greater range and inventiveness than ever before in his life. Painting pictures luminous and drab, towering and tiny, detailed still lifes and practically psychoanalytic flights of fantasy—as many as six or more in a single day. Nothing like this cornucopian outpouring has been known from any painter in the recorded history of art.

Because of the war these canvases were deposited in secret vaults of the Bank of France, protected from the invaders, never seen. Nothing of this period was sold during the Nazi occupation. For four years Picasso defied the Germans, continuing to live and paint as a Spanish " neutral " in the heart of Paris where he scorned the Gestapo to attend a memorial service for his old friend, Max Jacob, who had died in concentration camp. After liberation, when art market prices erupted to Vesuvian heights, it was unnecessary to sell from this hoard to meet expenses—almost the only motive inducing Picasso to part with a picture. This entire collection of pre-World War II paintings is still intact and in *La Californie*.

One extraordinary month when Picasso painted at least twenty-three major works is recreated here in its entirety (2 April - 2 May, 1936). There may have been other things produced in this period —engravings, drawings, etchings—but they are not stored with the canvases, and would not, in any case, be a part of this book. These twenty-three paintings are astonishing, to say the very least. They clearly reveal Picasso's genius for expressing exactly that which is in his artistic mind. This was an interval of troubled drifting in the surf of his private life. The paintings dissect his heart. I personally feel that this chapter of canvases will stand as one of the truly illuminating entries in art literature—if indeed we do care about the forces that drive a man of Picasso's stature. His is one of the most articulate voices to be heard in any medium, and these paintings permit even the least experienced of us to understand and share some of the pressures shaping Picasso's response, for they are forces that bear upon us all.

Again, in '37, we share Picasso's fable of the wounded Minotaur who is saved by a Muse with whom he falls in love, spending the rest of his days sitting on the shores of her sea while she floats atop the waves. We see the Riviera hill town of Mougins in its summer blaze of hollyhocks and sunshine. When word comes of disastrous reversals in Spain, the joyous colors of a Côte d'Azur holiday are translated into anguished women bewailing atrocities in Castile. Nuns rush blindly from their cloisters, too late. To keep his own sanity it seems that Picasso turned to loved faces around him, giving their portraits an inner flame which only the hand of a master artist could have lit. The simplest things

14

enchanted him and provided subjects for his brush—a plain ceramic urn, pastry brought from Cannes for lunch, thrushes twittering outside his window, his daughter playing with her sailboat. Then, as the conflict spread out of Spain and the world headed into another general war, Picasso's world exploded, too, and even the most beloved face became tortured and demented, with his canvases brutally reflecting the end of all tranquillity in his day-to-day life. These paintings are entirely unknown. Many are presented here in chronological order. Although they represent but a fraction of the total found and photographed in *La Californie* (sheer bulk of numbers and cost of reproducing them all in color prevent their being included), some of them, when known, will comprise whole chapters for one wishing to read them as another man's diary kept during some of the most violent years of this century—painted in passages as stark as those written by any pen.

Until now, or so I believe, no one has been able to provide the key for translating (the Rosetta Stone, if you wish) Picasso's most baffling paintings—also, perhaps, among his greatest—those of the tormented years that have shaped our existence since the First World War. He is one of the few artists who even attempted to express our times, after one gets beyond the poster painters who recruited many of us to meet the emergencies. Seen in their full, day by day chronological order, possible now in *La Californie* for the first time, where his total output of weeks on end is amassed, Picasso's paintings provide their own interpretations when, very simply, they are paired to the events directly affecting him, and our Earth, on their birth days. " Picasso? A man of the immediate moment!", appraises Daniel-Henry Kahnweiler, his dealer for over fifty years. His pictures tell their stories in diamond-hard terms, in symbols as clear as any I discovered earlier among the Kremlin treasures, which told the history of Russia. Picasso's art is not just more painting. The fragile thread of all our lives is the deeper theme.

Today, in his eightieth year, Picasso is still working steadily in his studio next to the room in *La Californie* where I have been copying his paintings from early morning until late at night. Many times I have found him standing quietly behind me awaiting the blaze of colors when my lights hit the canvas: " I'll only watch for a moment—I must keep ahead of you! " When I asked permission to switch his most recent pictures—a series of low-key portraits of Jacqueline—from his easel to mine I struck all but radiation from his eyes—explosive, palms-out, total refusal; one of the most absolute, ever. " No! They're not finished. You might take something away! " My astonishment was complete. It was the same profound, almost organic reaction that I had faced years before while photographing among desert tribesmen of Arabia and jungle tribesmen in South America. Both were convinced that the camera possessed the dreaded power of capturing their souls. Picasso was protecting his paintings until they were mature, until they should enter the outside world, there to fend for themselves. In this moment I felt perhaps closer to the Maestro than at any time during all of our days together. And more remote, for I again faced the question that had haunted me since long before we met . . .

Who is Pablo Picasso...

Who is this man
with a fighter's shoulders
who has turned his back upon most of the artistic traditions
of his own or any time;
whose joys and sorrows,
whose dreams
are slowly becoming a language spoken by others,
given to them by another of those rare men
who seek alone.

Who
is this man
who
can turn any tool,
any color,
all material,
to his needs;
whose eyes
simply see more
than those of other men—
whose eyes
have offered deeper vision
to us all.

Who is this man
to whom the meaning
of " life " and " art "
is the same;
who sees space
and surface
as challenges
to be met in combat
upon those broad plains
of the imagination
where his own hand
rules supreme.

Who is this man
whose silence is so commanding
no one violates the frontier of his mind
when he journeys to the land of his visions
seeking new faces to populate that world which he created,
where, even today, other travellers are almost unknown.

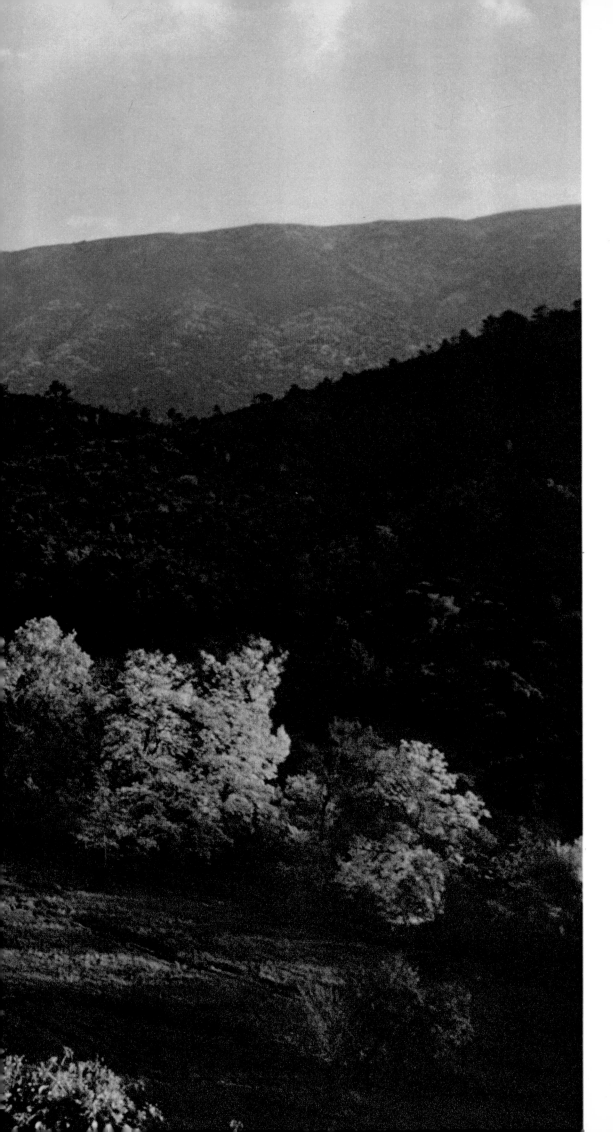

Who is this man
who moved deep
into the hills
of Cézanne,
among the rolling hills
feeding the heights
of Mount Sainte-Victoire;
within time-embattled walls
of a fortress-chateau
called *Vauvenargues*.
But then,
although the elements
emblazoned the heavens
with their welcome,
his eyes
already were seeking
new horizons
far beyond rainbows
or the mere heights
of Sainte-Victoire.

29

Who is this man
who sees all of life as a stage;
and yet,
even as he stands silently watching,
he himself is playing a major part.

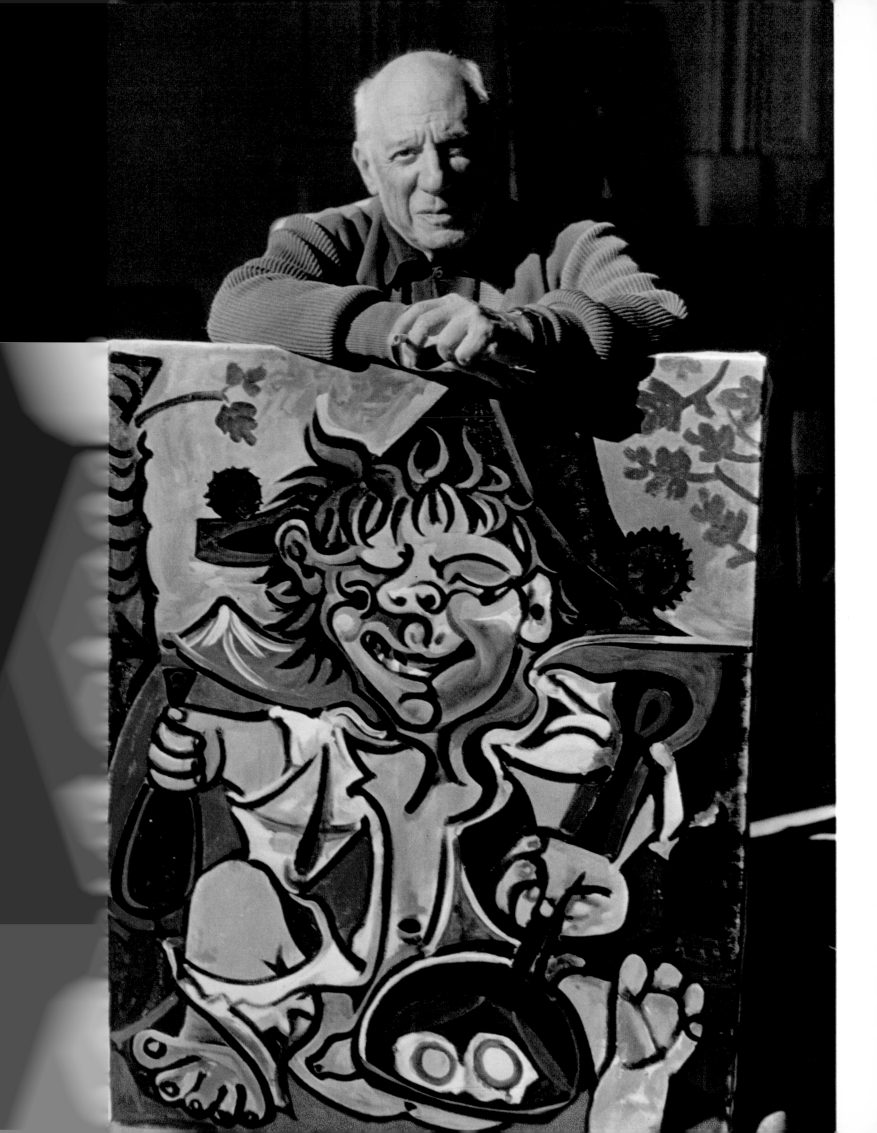

. . . cloaked and somber as any duke of Castile . . . at work in *La Californie's* gypsy clutter . . . humorously sketching rowdy Bacchanalian scenes . . . reflective beneath the fortress austerity of *Vauvenargues*: these are but fleeting glimpses of Picasso today, the benign genie who is far too mercurial to be trapped by any lens. Many times my photo coverage of him appeared complete, when unseen facets of his character began winking provocatively—sometimes elusively—before other lights and lenses. His portrait of the *Urchin of Vauvenargues* is the same—simply a tousled, mischievous Spanish child wandering alone over life's mountain paths—until one looks again. Magically, three roguish children (right and left profiles, and full face) then burst into laughter upon the canvas.

During this last year, while living among hundreds of Picassos, the Maestro himself has seemed to mask far more than just three bright-eyed wanderers who have constantly roamed unexplored trails among the peaks, painting the stories of each discovery and dream revealed along the way. And it is only here, by following the slashing strokes of a brush that has dueled for a lifetime down in those narrow streets where Man is his most violent, or by listening to a heart-song dedicated as purely to love as love itself has ever been; only by searching here—often among carnival colors of great canvases aflame—will anyone ever answer . . . Who is Pablo Picasso?

Picasso's Picassos

1895-1960

Late in the autumn of 1895 an obscure professor of art, José Ruiz Blasco, settled his family in the sunny warmth of Barcelona after moving across Spain from La Coruña on the rainy northwest coast. Shortly thereafter, a deeply religious picture came from the easel of his son, Pablo Ruiz Picasso. It was this *Flight to Egypt*, in which the Holy Family seems to be truly a part of the Palestinian scene. Having spent many years in the Middle East as a foreign correspondent, I asked Picasso where he had seen such simple adobe homes as that in the background of the canvas, for nothing like it exists in Spain. He only shrugged. Then I asked about the curious image floating in the sky above Jesus' Mother—speculating that it might be the Holy Spirit. " Holy Spirit! " Picasso's snort was explosive, and a bit derisive, too, as though I really was not too familiar with the Bible Land. " Those are dates! That's a palm tree—with dates. They had to eat *something!* " At the time he painted the picture, the Maestro was fourteen.

1895

19 ³/₄ × 14 ¹/₄

1895/1896   *7 1/4 × 9 1/8*

The Barcelona which Picasso knew as a youth fills him with nostalgia even today. His most intimate comrades were those of the early years when life and its conquests still lay ahead, when faith in his gift as an artist flowed from only one inexhaustible source—himself. Now, while viewing paintings from that first, unnamed period of his career, Picasso greets them with a special warmth, as though his oldest friends have come back to visit. Except for some classical, extremely rare religious canvases, the bulk of his output dealt with the same ever-turbulent, multi-hued theme . . . Barcelona and her peoples, who had engulfed him. It was a city where sidewalks were lined with portable shrines on saints' days, with young girls of each district soliciting donations from passersby. Picasso chuckled with gentle amusement when he saw the film of this painting projected—almost as though he was again watching the scene from across the street. " But look how properly they are dressed, and how graciously he is handing the girl his peseta—even though it probably is his last! "

1895/1896

23 ³/₄ × 28

44

-. 4. 1896   8 ⁷/₈ × 13

Most of Picasso's earliest works, now in the world's great museums and private collections, are renowned for their piercing outcry against the endemic social injustice that once choked Barcelona's mournful backstreets, the stage of his youth.   Hidden away, unknown until now, a few still older canvases have survived to reveal another, utterly romantic side of the Maestro's childhood scene.   One shows sunlit fields, sentinel cypresses and gaily gowned beauties flouncing along in ritual procession toward an ancient chapel outside of town.   Another, with wry humor, is of a delicately veiled señorita and her bridesmaid—on their way to the altar—turning in astonishment to watch as her recently betrothed suffers a last minute change of heart, and bolts for the door.

45

"Once, this picture was big, really big." Picasso's sweeping gesture indicated a canvas that would have towered above my head. "But that was long ago. I later painted it over with other subjects many times, then cut it to pieces and then painted again. This is all that remains. It is my father."

1897/1898

7 1/4 × 5 1/2

1899   *18 ¹/₈ × 21 ⁵/₈*

There was nothing genteel about the neighborhood of Barcelona where Picasso fought to survive after first leaving home to paint alone. It was a shadow world of prostitutes and lurching seamen, gas-lit cabarets and faces without names drifting through the gloom—one in which a girl, who could find no conveniences in a place among the worst, went out into the night, then returned to the lights rearranging herself as best she could. Now, looking back at her over the cushioning years, even Picasso seems shocked—not entirely by the picture, perhaps, but that she could have existed like this, at all—and shakes his head in disbelief while exclaiming to his wife, Jacqueline, " But how could I ever have painted *that!* "

49

In the generally lyric realm of the female nude in art five grotesque girls known as *Les Demoiselles d'Avignon* are probably among the most celebrated, even though unsurpassed in their lack of feminine charms. Picasso painted them in mid-1907, in a canvas so bizarre that his closest friends were first stunned, then vehemently critical of the liberties he had taken with the heretofore nearly sacred human figure. Picasso neither explained nor defended it, but just left the massive work rolled in a corner of his studio. It remained ignored for years before finally travelling to New York to be hung alone on a special wall of its own. There, like the Black Stone in the Great Mosque of Mecca, it is now acclaimed by all pilgrims paying homage at one of the major shrines of modern art.

One morning, while arranging my day's shooting in *La Californie*, I found this incredible portrait sandwiched between several still lifes of a much later era. Painted on a panel so thin that it is nearly transparent (the lid of an ancient paint box) it seems as though the colors merely screen the person behind. The face itself is one of *Les Demoiselles d'Avignon*—with several remarkable differences, the most conspicuous being her red hair. Picasso has often told me that his father was a red-bearded giant, " Much taller than even you ", (putting him well over six feet). Numerous descriptions have been written about the Maestro's " burning black eyes "—which do have an inner fire of their own but are chestnut of precisely the shade as those staring out from the panel. Yet it is the searching, ever-wistful appeal in this face that made Jacqueline smile in agreement with me when I turned to Picasso with no question in my voice, " Of course, this is you, too. In every way, it is you. " For a moment he said nothing while his eyes bored into the projected image on the screen. Then his cigarette glowed in the darkened studio. " It was painted several months before *Les Demoiselles d'Avignon*, in the winter, around the beginning of 1907 . . . see me here if you wish—but it was not intended. "

1907

10 $^1/_8$ × 6 $^5/_8$

1907/1908   6 1/8 × 7

During the first years of this century, who knows what chords were sounded upon the strings of the instrument which is Picasso, after he discovered the moldering masks and dust-coated ceremonial idols of Black Africa heaped in long-neglected tangles in the ethnological department of the Museum of Man in Paris—yet a few of the notes would vibrate within his own artistic language throughout life.

Once, while discussing traces of El Greco and Cézanne seen in some of his earlier pictures, Picasso had rumbled impatiently, in his bass fiddle voice, " Naturally! Every painter must have a father and a mother. "

52

1907/1908

$7 \times 5 \frac{5}{8}$

1908

10 5/8 × 8 3/...

54

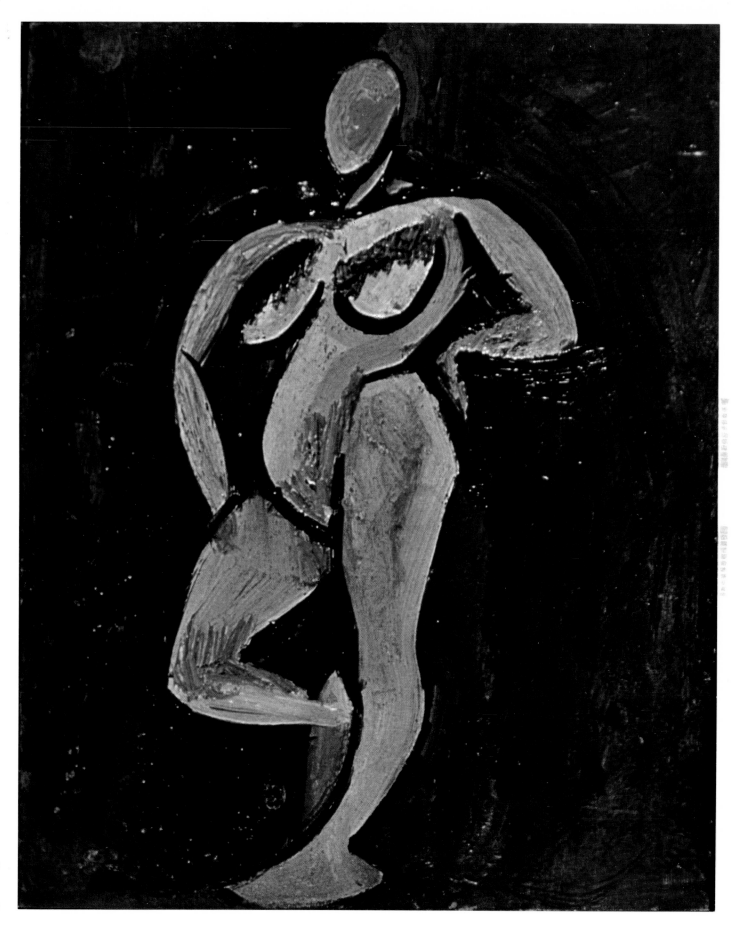

1908

10 ⁵/₈ × 8 ³/₈

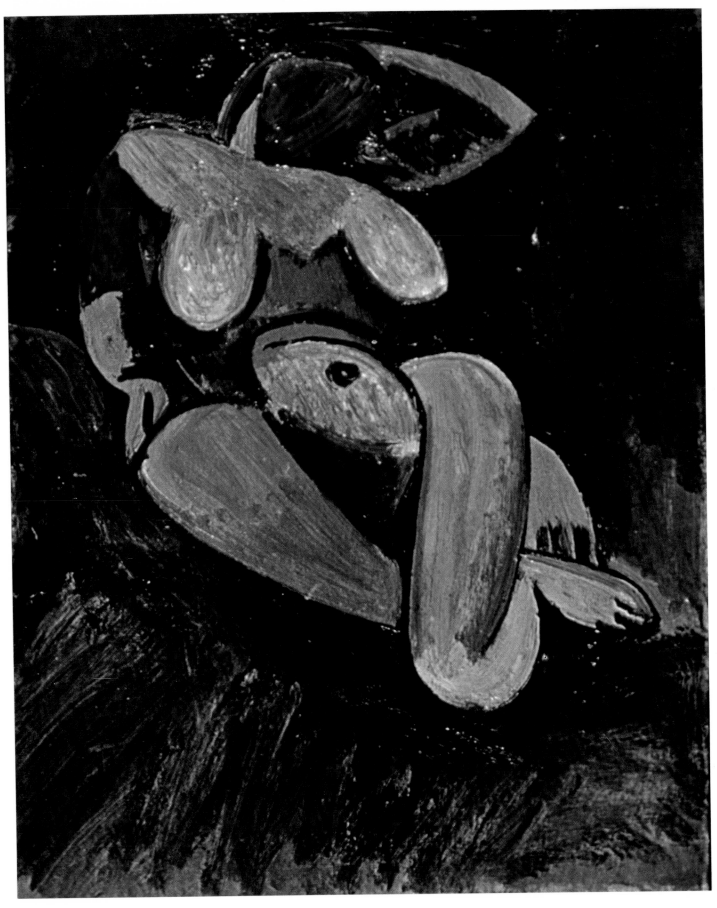

1908

10 ⁵/₈ × 8 ³/₈

1908 $8\,^3/_8 \times 10\,^5/_8$

1908

$8\,^3/_8 \times 10\,^5/_8$

Many artists' influences surrounded Picasso during the first decade of this century; paintings of the long-gone Renaissance and of the Spanish court, and of the French Impressionists from the more recent past; primitive sculpture of Africa, found in Paris museums—and the legacy of Paul Cézanne. The Maestro's phenomenal power of instant assimilation of objects beneath his gaze is already legendary and pertains to all things except Cézanne, who inspired him in his youth and continues to provide challenges of understanding even today when he commands total response from his own creative genius. If Picasso were to reply (most unlikely) to the question of naming his favorite painter, I should guess it would be Cézanne.

One day, a collector brought a portrait of Cézanne's wife to *La Californie* hoping the Maestro would buy it or, even better, trade it for one of his own canvases. The painting had scarcely been unwrapped before Picasso turned to speak with other guests in the room. Cézanne's wife stood abandoned, it seemed. Suddenly Picasso spun around practically with tears of anger in his eyes, and blurted, " Poor Cézanne! Where *is* Cézanne? Museums and dealers are monsters—nothing remains but varnish. She's been cleaned to the bone. Why not do it to your car? ", looking straight at me, as though it was my fault. " And they *already* do it to my pictures! Where is the hand of poor Cézanne? "

Sometime between 1908 and 1909, with *Les Demoiselles d'Avignon* more than a year old and African-influenced canvases nearly overflowing his studio, Picasso—retaining his palette of greys, greens, chocolate and cobalt—turned first to Cézanne's cryptic brush strokes, then to his magic formula of recreating the visual world into cylinders, spheres and cones. Picasso and Georges Braque, originally painting independently of each other, were soon embarked upon a voyage of easel experiments whereby *their* visual world—architecture, landscape, the human figure—would be progressively reduced to its ultimate factor. Seeking still further to create an illusion *in space* on the surface of their canvases, they simplified their subjects to semi-objective, three-dimensional planes—thus giving birth to the force destined to liberate all figurative painting from its past.

This small panel of two bathers drying themselves below their house on a rock-strewn shore represents one of the first steps taken by an infant group born under the brand of a single word— Cubist. Cubism, and the rigid austerity which it imposed upon its practioners in such related arts as sculpture and architecture, was destined to be the mold that shaped the features of Man's major efforts in self-expression during the first half of the twentieth century.

908/1909

8 × 8 3/8

1908/1909

$10\,^5/_8 \times 8\,^3/_8$

1908/1909

$9 \; ^5/_8 \times 8 \; ^3/_8$

1908/1909

10 ⁵/₈ × 8 ³/₈

1909

$10 \, ^5/_8 \times 8 \, ^3/_8$

1918

32 ¹/₂ × 46 ³/

For days after photographing this Cubist watchdog peering from his kennel, I found real pleasure in leaving him near my cameras to greet me again each morning when I arrived at *La Californie* to work. He seemed remarkably like Kublai Khan, a droll Afghan who frolicked around my home in Rome. When checking the photographs of the painting with Picasso, I casually mentioned what good company the hound had been during my long hours alone in the villa's attic. The Maestro looked around apparently thinking I meant one of *his* dogs, who chase each other tirelessly through the house. Then, slowly, unbelievingly, he swung those eyes at me. " Hound? . . . *hound!* Dooncan, this is a table, with a table cloth. There is a guitar at the left. And a pitcher at the right. You *must* see that! " For him there was no question, nor was there for Jacqueline; they saw the table and its contents instantly. I never confessed but I still saw Kublai, too—and was very happy. It reminded me of those cloud games where my brothers and I as children found fantastic faces among thunderheads piled high in summer skies. For each of us the discoveries were different—which detracted nothing at all from our joy.

70

1919

51 ^{1}/$_8$ × 35

Several new facets were burnished into Picasso's life during a 1917 trip to Rome to design scenery and costumes for the premier performance of *Parade*, an avant-garde production staged by Diaghilev's Russian Ballet. The ballet itself proved a disaster when it opened later in Paris—the audience apparently stopped just short of demanding public guillotining for all concerned. But for the Maestro, the Italian journey was profoundly rewarding. After ten intense years of simultaneous invention and evolution within the cell-like limitations of Cubism, he was catapulted into the provocative atmosphere of Jean Cocteau's writing, Erik Satie's music, Diaghilev's choreography, Leonid Massine's dancing—and the girls of the corps de ballet. One of them, Olga Koklova, was to become his wife and the mother of Paulo, his first child.

Italy's nearly timeless artistic traditions—and the giants who created them—sparked a sympathetic response within Picasso that would continue to surface periodically throughout each decade as he stood before his easel. These works, generally portraits of persons whom he loved or most admired, show great attention given to subtle refinements in color, supported by a master draftsman's contempt for superfluous lines. As with all others of Picasso's studio moods, which he himself *never* names or identifies, these Italian-inspired canvases have been catalogued and labelled, rather romantically, as Neo-Classic. This miniature yet monumental nude, had it been known before, might have prompted the label-makers into conjuring up still another name—Heroic.

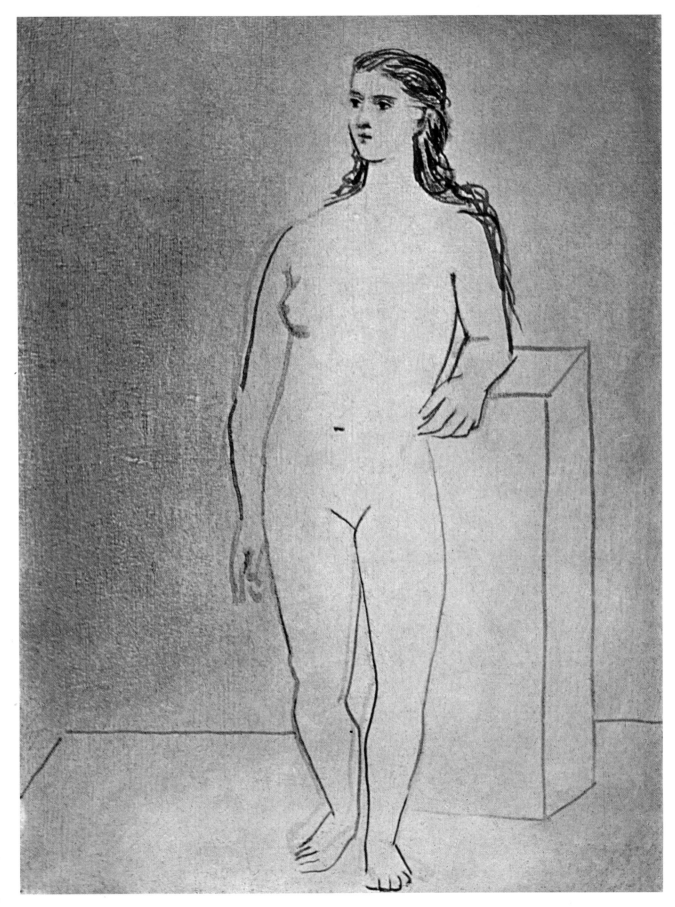

7. 11. 1923

13 × 9 ¹/₂

Paulo had just celebrated his fourth birthday when the Maestro, barely touching the canvas with his brush, painted this portrait of his son—a picture that clearly reveals the sophistication with which Olga Picasso hoped to clothe her family. The socially conscious daughter of a general in the Tzarist Army, she must have had considerable difficulty adjusting to the studied chaos and bohemian friends with which her husband surrounded himself. None of the many portraits painted of Paulo throughout his childhood mirror anything of the backstreets of Barcelona or Paris which his father knew as a child. Picasso himself, who is about as socially aspiring as a gypsy, must have viewed the obligations of rising fame and well-being as gross affronts to his privacy; to contend with additional infringements within his own home must surely have been an ordeal.

Once, while having a bouillabaisse dinner with Jacqueline and the Maestro in St. Tropez, I asked whether there was more understanding today of his work than when he was painting Cubist and Blue Period pictures, fighting obscurity and privation. Jacqueline stared in astonishment while, for the first time ever in their presence, I wrote his reply in my notebook instead of waiting until later trusting my training as a journalist to remember it: " Now? Much less. Now there is fame! Of all—hunger, misery, the incomprehension by the public—fame is by far the worst. It is the castigation by God of the artist. It is sad. It is true. "

More than three months later, standing beside me as I copied a painting, Picasso supplied the other half of his comment at St. Tropez. He had just turned away a Dutch photographer who had come with an introduction from a major contemporary sculptor to ask permission to shoot a reportage on Picasso, the sculptor. Before departing, the guest had left an enormous box of the finest Swiss chocolates. Now, Picasso's legs seemed driven into the floor, riveted there, as though he was burdened with an unbearable load. " Everyone brings me chorizos and cakes—everything! If only they would give me tranquility! It would be the greatest thing. But no one ever does because it costs nothing. *Everyone* is good! He is really a good photographer. All the world is good and I'm bad. Maybe it would be better if they all were bad and I good. It would be so much easier to work. "

9. 2. 1925

$9 \, ^1/_2 \times 6 \, ^1/_4$

Who knows what was in Picasso's mind when he painted this girl on the beach at Dinard, but the minuscule canvas could have come from no other hand.

Late one night, after having supper with the Maestro and Jacqueline in the kitchen of *La Californie*, I saw some of his paintings of the previous week; wooden panels where other-world couples were lazily sunning themselves on nearby beaches. During the meal I mentioned that it seemed really eerie to me to watch his gaze leap from article to article on the table and around the room, knowing perfectly well he was not seeing *anything* as I saw it, and never had. I added that it seemed incredible that one person ever dreamed of such varied images throughout a lifetime and could still be doing it today apparently without even trying. Picasso answered very simply. " If I had *tried*, they would all look the same."

23. 8. 1929 $6\,^1/_4 \times 8\,^5/_8$

2 April... 1936 ...2 May

Picasso has long been a paradox and enigma to even his oldest acquaintances; a gregarious friend, devoted to Olympian isolation; practically unschooled, yet literate to a mystic degree; loquacious, but obviously happy when submerged in Trappist silence; homespun, though so familiar with the myths of ancient gods that their lore and his seem entwined . . . a friend who has shared all others' innermost secrets and been the pivot for many of their lives, while himself always shielding dreams in the limitless preserves of a mind where no one else may tread.

During the middle years of the '30s, with Hitler, Mussolini and Tojo stoking fires that would soon sear the earth, Picasso's personal world overflowed with suffering, too, for his home was shattered when his marriage collapsed under forces no one could control. Olga's health and his own seemed broken— all sounds in the great studio were stilled. Each time friends called the shock was the same—Picasso, the painter, was now Picasso, the poet—neither brush nor fresh canvas could be seen.

In one of the most definitive books on the Maestro yet written, *Picasso: Fifty Years of His Art*, Alfred H. Barr, Jr. states: "The *Interior with a Girl Drawing* occupies a special place in Picasso's work of the midthirties for not only is it the culmination of the long series of similar subjects which he began in 1934 but it is apparently the last important canvas he painted until early 1937, a period of almost two years... Whatever reasons may have caused Picasso to stop painting early in 1935—and they seem to have been personal and circumstantial—his creative energies for some twenty months thereafter were to find expression in graphic art and poetry, though the results were meager by comparison with any previous period of similar length. During his long fallow period Picasso drew closer to the Surrealists, particularly the poets . . . "

Neither Barr nor anyone else could have known—because the Maestro never confided from the depths of his secretive Spanish heart—that some of the most varied works ever to come from his easel were created during this long, gloom-smitten, " fallow " period. They were soon stacked in separate strong-rooms, racked with other paintings by size—not by date—thus no one, including Pablo Picasso, has until now seen these pictures grouped together since the month when twenty-three of them were born.

Marie-Thérèse . . . the blonde, classic-profiled wanderer upon the Maestro's troubled shores; part moon goddess—half earthly mate, after the wrenching end of marriage, a welcomed hand of escape: Picasso's inspiration for many of the serenely painted portraits that will help mark his place in art.

2 Avril XXXVI

936

8 1/8

3.

21

82

1936

× 15

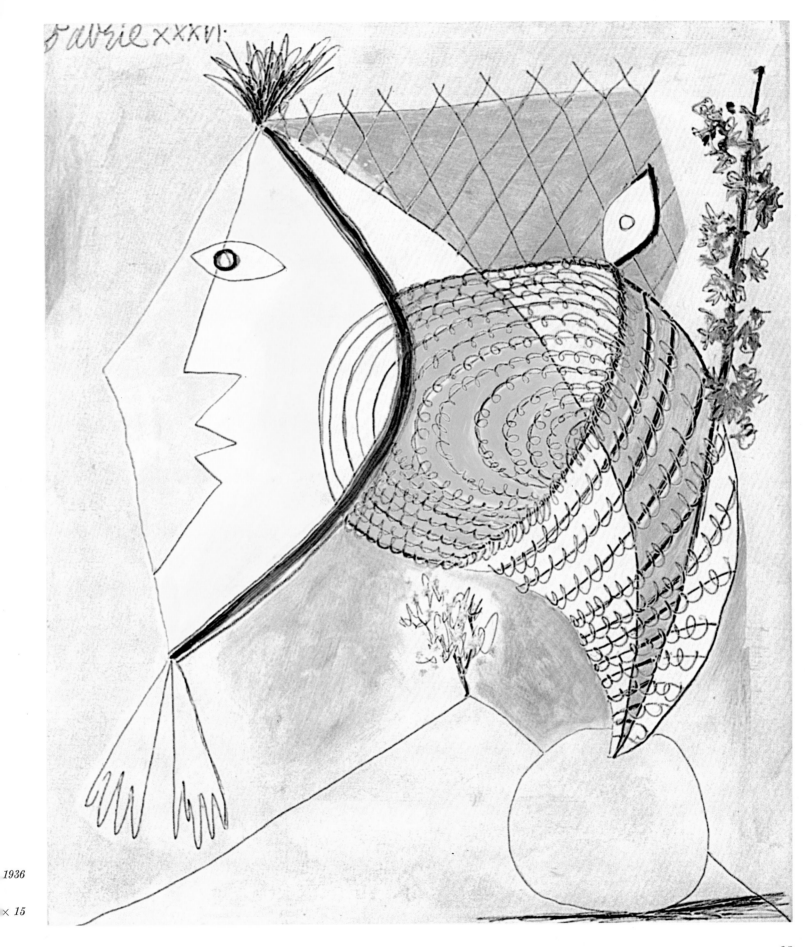

5 avril XXXVI.

1936

× 15

85

6. 4. 1936

$18\,^{1}/_{8} \times 21\,^{5}/_{8}$

Minotaur, half man, half beast—born of violence in the mythology of ancient Crete—appeared in the pantheon of Picasso's world when his personal life was in turmoil, when there must have seemed no way out. Years ago a single drawing of this subject became known, which some almost psychic person titled *Minotaur Moving His House*. Recently, while checking my transparencies of this painting with the Maestro, I pointed to the incredible load piled upon the cart, especially to the multi-colored ribbons which I saw as a matador's banderillas that had been tossed in, along with his picador's gored horse. "Banderillas!" Picasso's snort told me that again I was wrong. "It's a painting, in a frame, which he won't leave behind. And the horse isn't gored—she's having a baby! Now, do you see the tiny head, and the little red feet—*now*, do you see the child?"

In the Maestro's new home, sparsely furnished with a few old things that had travelled with him from the start, the tide of life had caught him on its crest and was carrying him forward once more.

9. 4. 19

21 $^5/_8$ ×

88

1936

19 5/8

13. 4

25 ⁵/

Portraits of Marie-Thérèse flowed from Picasso's easel—sometimes more than one a day—which now serve as pass-keys into his often perplexing style. Reminiscent of the exploratory days of Cubism when he sought new ways of paring down each subject to an ultimate visual factor, the Maestro now worked with this one face to express its secret within a vivid spider-work of lines. He also left clues for tracing the steps by which his pictures are formed. " Someday, later, " he once observed while I was copying his marks on the back of a canvas, " someone may be curious—he may want to know. That is why I now date everything I touch. "

His first painting is generally the most detailed, the nearest to reality. Successively thereafter, if he continues, the subject is reduced to its minimal recognizable form. Astonishingly, by distillation the essence of each subject's character is often brought to light.

Seeking still more than an easy-for-him portrait within the tracery of Marie-Thérèse's features and the person he saw there, Picasso—foregoing any attempt at beauty as beauty is generally known—may here have probed deeper, to the very heart of Creation, into the womb where life ignites life . . . to the actual splitting of the cell—the source of all beauty, and life itself.

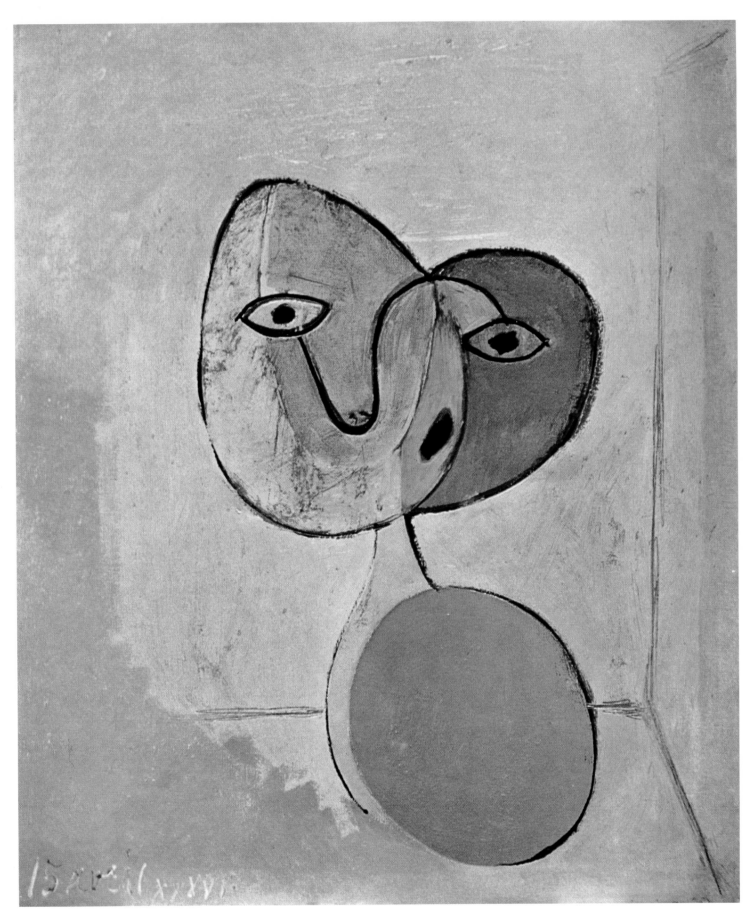

4. 1936

× 19 5/8

A bowl of fruit, flowers in their vase, a loaf of bread—commonplace things in any French house—painted by Picasso as though he had looked back, almost with surprise, upon finding them in this new home of his own.

1936

23 ⁵/₈

17. 4. 1

28 ³/₄ ⟩

Awaiting her time—arranging a simple bouquet in a pitcher—softly billowing with all the ripened curves of fertility; the aching, pollinated human flower . . . awaiting her time.

0. 4. 1936

6 1/8 × 13

22.

18 ¹

24 avril XXXVI

936

1/4

25. 4. 1936

21 $^1/_4$ × 25 $^5/_8$

25. 4.

18 ¹/₈

30

25

One afternoon, the Maestro lingered for a moment beside me before going into his studio to work. As we were climbing the villa's massive staircase after lunch I had been thinking of a picture copied earlier, of a wretched brunette woman seated on the floor of a windowless room. She stared into a darkening mirror, as garlands of withered flowers dangled from her hair. A comb had fallen to the cushion beside her. Dully admiring her faded image she did not know that beauty had fled. I again placed the canvas upon my easel and told Picasso it was the saddest painting I had ever seen. The Maestro looked just for an instant, then muttered, " That was the worst time of my life. "

1. 5. 1

24 ×

5. 1936

19 5/8

All garlands gone, her watch forgotten—lost in a land where each day seemed the same—a woman, unaware of the visitor who now shared her room, sat watching shadows in a blackened mirror where nothing could be seen.

22. 12. 1936 I   *10 ⁵/₈ × 16 ¹/₈*

Fantasy and reality: a purely imaginary still life becomes more real than an entirely real collage—which becomes the more fantastic. Both are expressions in Picasso's idiom as he speaks of things nearby. While I was photographing this collage—a box as the wine bottle, steel-wool as the fruit, odds and ends as the glass, knife and platter, a table cloth as the table cloth—the Maestro came from his studio to stand beside me. More than an hour passed. Despite all efforts I could never light its contours without reflections blinding my lens. Finally, frustrated, half-infuriated by the contraption, I shoved my great lights practically behind the easel and headed for the lens, when a thunderous slap across the back spun me right around. " *Now* we see it's not a painting! It was only for this that I made it. Now, it's *really* not the same! "

116

-. 2. 1937   19 $^5/_8$ × 25 $^5/_8$

No troubadour ever sang his ballads with more variations than has Picasso in his portraits. By 1937 their flow had risen until a geyser was showering canvases from his easel, as many as six a day. In them he created a shining world of love and innocence—of a place which his own romantic heart had never known—and gave it with a flourish to the almost mystic girl who now shared his home. Neither cloistered princess, nor feted heroine, not even Lancelot's Guinevere was more regally cloaked in sables and lace or crowned in gems so pure as the single spray of lilacs with which he jewelled Marie-Thérèse's hair.

1937

23 ⁵/₈

3. 2.

28 ³/₄

4. 2. 1937

36 ¹/₄ × 25 ⁵/₈

11. 3. 1937

51 ¹/₈ × 38 ¹/₈

19. 6. 1937   6 ¼ × 8 ⁸

When Picasso painted *Guernica*—his silently shrieking monument to fellow Spaniards massacred in their market place by Nazi pilots casually practicing bombing—he filled three hundred square feet of canvas with lightning bolts and thunder saying all that he knew about dying, and more than anyone had ever said about war. Yet no one can live on just anger, or survive without a dream, so he turned to his own plain table and to the girl serenely sitting beside him, to paint offerings of food as though upon an altar—and a goddess of mercy for others wounded along the way.

24. 6. 1937

18 $^1/_8$ × 13

6. 9. 1937 II

23 ⁵/₈ × 31 ⁷/₈

Blazing Mediterranean sunshine and the summer circus colors of his then favorite Riviera hill town, Mougins, had just welcomed Picasso and his friends to another vacation, when news from Spain laid the dead of that war right beside his door.   Immediately, his paint seemed scorched by the rage of men whose blood was the first to fall.   Then his canvas mirrored their women, silently weeping—standing next in line against the wall.

8. 9. 1937 II

31 $^7/_8$ × 23 $^5/_8$

130

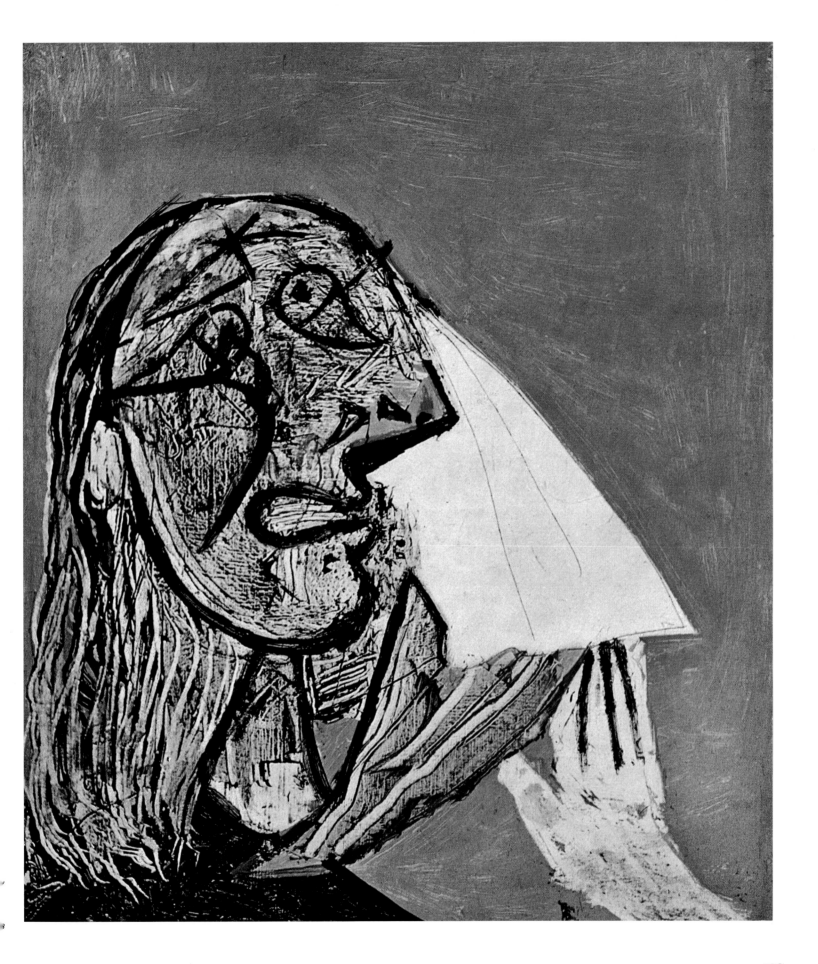

For several days, late in 1937, after months of disastrous news from Spain, the Maestro seemed lured to siren shores enraptured by singing which only he could hear. Among those who beckoned, his gaze met that of an aquamarine girl with sapphire eyes, and a moon shadow silhouetted by flaxen hair.

Looking back the next morning as he sailed from the shore, he searched for the face of the night before. He was greeted instead by the piercing glare from a single eye. It was no moon shadowed girl who had smiled in the night, but her Cyclopean queen whose other eye was now ice.

. 1937

19 5/8

18. 12. 1937

$9\ ^1/_2 \times 7\ ^1/_2$

138

Anyone wishing to decipher Picasso's often perplexing paintings generally has but to correlate the date of a canvas to world news or to events in his personal life on that day, at which time one frequently would be navigating through emotional currents as turbulent as whirlpools in a hurricane sea.

When 1937 ended with even more horror in Spain, Picasso's easel became haunted by dying horses, murdered children, ravaged nuns, and someone's never-pretty maiden aunt fleeing her loom. Its spindles were fingers, bare to the bones. Though her breast was blasted open she was unaware of her wounds. Yet she knew, in this moment as with all of her life, there was no one to cry for. Now it was too late.

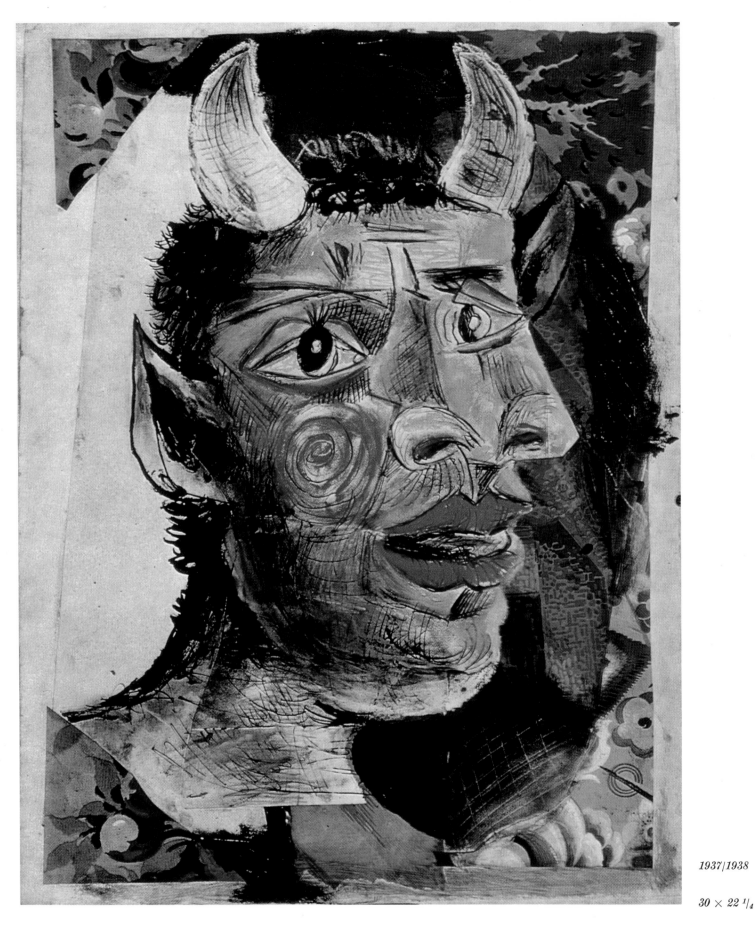

1937/1938

30 × 22 ¹/₄

140

31. 12. 1937

18 ⅛ × 21 ⅝

Once, while most of the world was celebrating a new year, Picasso stood before his easel painting a fable; one of violence, yet of love, too, where the Minotaur lay dying, clutching the sand. Three Muses sailing nearby discovered the monster sprawled on the beach. Two fled the grisly sight, but one stayed to do what she might to save the dread creature just beyond reach, who, when she called, struggled upright. Yet he needed first wine then her mirror to make himself well. Forever thereafter, while she floated off shore, he spent his days sitting where she had offered the only love he had found in life.

1. 1. 1938

18 $^1/_8$ × 21 $^5/_8$

. 1. 1938

19 5/8 × 24

Many art critics have attempted to rationalize Picasso's use of single-plane distortion in portraits. One regards it as the application of a formula similar to Mercator's Projection, which accomodated itself to the curvature of the earth and which now is accepted by many as the *actual* appearance of our world. Another relates it to the earlier voyages into the mysteries of Cubism which the Maestro and Braque investigated in their youth. Actually, it may be just possible that Picasso's world is revolving solely around an extreme example of subjective vision made tangible by a God-given talent for expressing himself in a language that he had to invent.

Now, after living for several years among hundreds of Picasso portraits—like this of Marie-Thérèse and others of her daughter Maia—covering all the years of his career, I find that I demand far more of pictures and probe deeper for hidden life. It is also easier to answer the sometimes scoffing question from those hearing of my welcome in Picasso's home, who ask what it is that I find in distortions that violate centuries of traditions in painting, when most art was conceived as beauty dedicated to God in Mankind's name. Regarding beauty, the answer is easy: as in love, its secret is the secret of the smitten. But regarding our artistic traditions, the answer can only be posed as a question: what artist living during the root centuries of Western art—Greek or Roman, Byzantine or Renaissance, Gothic or Flemish—what artist, *anywhere*, ever saw an aureole of laughing, bodyless cherubs, haloed martyrs, or winged saints— those sacred clichés of classical religious art, distortions themselves, which now are considered inviolable.

144

9·1·38·

22.

25.

146

30. 1. 1938

24 × 18 ¹/₈

6. 3. 1938

$7 ^1/_2 \times 9 ^1/_2$

150

Not only do Picasso's paintings reflect world crises and the sometimes nearly unbearable strains within life itself, but also an acute sensitivity to Nature's great easel—to the way *she* paints our earth.

Summertime: lush, cricket-choired, blossom-heavy, promenade-provoking summertime . . . Dora Maar, in her new bonnet; Paris, in mid-summer. When I mentioned to Picasso that this and a companion portrait of the following week were among my favorites of all the paintings I had photographed, he just looked at them and shrugged; but then, with a puckish grin, turned and said, " Of course, if she really had walked around in that blouse she would have spent summer in jail. "

1938

23 5/8

153

1938

$9\,{}^{1}/_{2} \times 7\,{}^{1}/_{2}$

154

27. 11. 1938

28 ³/₄ × 36 ¹/₄

Maia, the Maestro's daughter, watching winter's first storm—a portrait so delicate it seems almost to be painted with the snow itself. In a nearby still life of an artist's studio with its burning candle, poised palette and waiting frame—dominated by a flaming statue of the great Minotaur himself—one discovers a veined scratch lacing one edge of the canvas opposite the candle, curiously balancing its light. Picasso surely would be the last to repair it, probably grunting instead, " ¡ *Tanto mejor!* " . . . " So much the better! " Once, when he saw me feather-brushing a painting clean he stopped me. " Leave the dust—it's a part of me, too. Besides, it helps protect the colors. " He does not laugh when he says that nothing in art has served him better than dust.

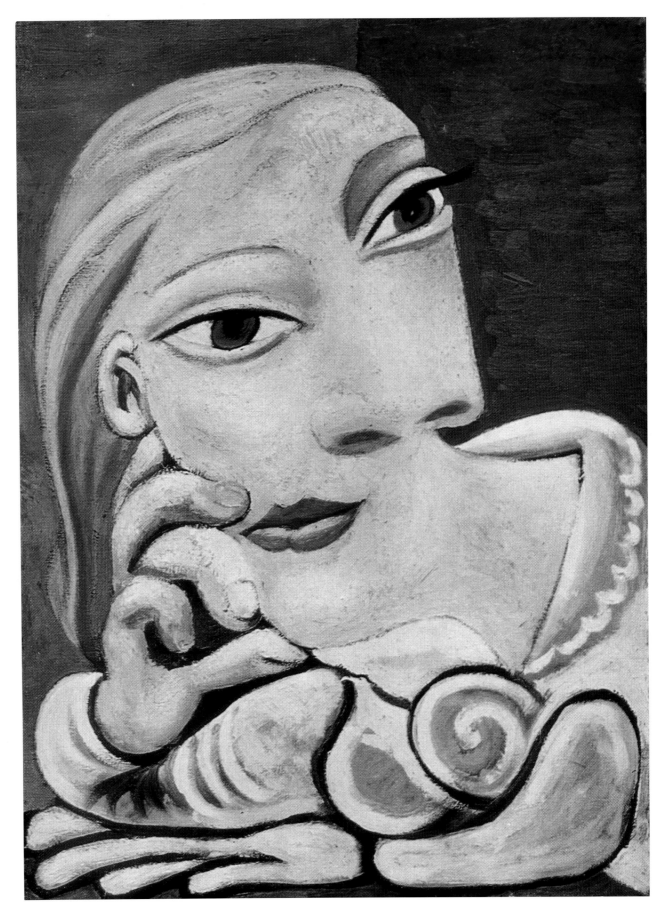

7. 1. 1939

25 5/8 × 18 1/8

*. 1939

x 31⁷/₈

12. 2. 1939   *5 ¹/₂ × 7 ¹/₂*

As a photographer, after many months of handling armloads of pictures in *La Californie*, one aspect of Picasso's work impressed me perhaps more than any other. This was his seemingly unerring sense of composition and scale while working within the rigid frame of his canvas, whether painting monolithic murals or miniatures of birds and flowers. Having shot *my* world for a lifetime through the viewfinder of a camera—recording values that had to be quickly seen and caught, or forever lost, within the restrictive framework of that finder—I felt that I was communicating with a kindred soul when I saw what he had sought and caught . . . and yet, deep in my heart, I wondered whether he, too, had ever lost.

22. 2. 1939

7 $^1/_2$ × 5 $^1/_2$

One night, several months after photographing Picasso's Picassos in *La Californie*—after more than five hundred different canvases of every shape, subject, size and color had passed before my easel—and several weeks before even a preliminary selection of paintings for this book had been made, an extraordinarily vivid dream ripped through my sleep. I had been walking alone through a dark pine forest following the turns of a sandy trail. No sound came from the shadowy depths, yet it was a peaceful place with no hint of gloom. The trees opened suddenly to form a natural room into which, from the left, ran a path through wild flowers starting to bloom. As I hesitated, undecided whether to turn, a hellish thrashing shattered the calm, uprooting the flowers at the point where the two paths joined. I reached for my camera and headed for the noise, then stopped, for just before me, her head twisted toward the sky, an epileptic girl stood gasping, hoping her seizure would subside. The moment it passed, when the glen was again quiet, she lingered for a moment; then scurrying through the flowers she disappeared down the trail, with a wisp of a dog running at her side.

Though astonishingly clear, the dream was made even more unforgettable because out of the entire *flow* of action which comprised the sequence, a single image remained transfixed in my memory the next morning, rigidly frozen and detailed, as though I had shot it with stroboscopic flash. It was this picture by Picasso of a grisly woman stricken by some horrendous, body-wracking malady. He painted it in the spring of 1939, after Czechoslovakia had fallen, Austria was gone, and Hitler was preparing to march on the world after Munich.

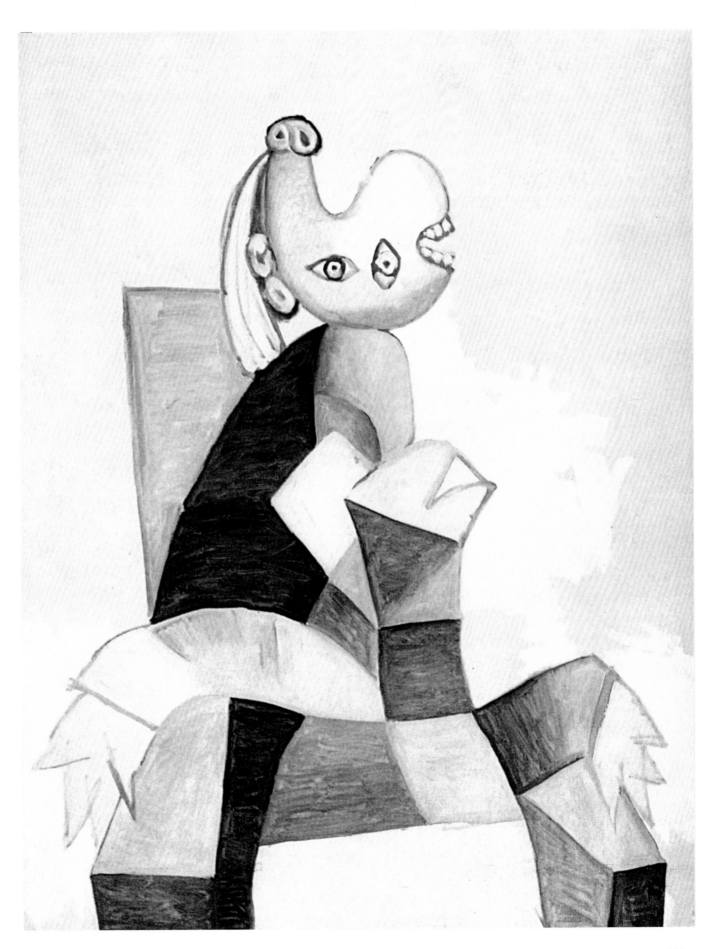

1. 4. 1939

51 ¹/₈ × 38 ¹/₈

Even as Nature is subject to the whims of her seasons, the artist most certainly must be borne along by the ebb and flow of the emotional tides of that world in which he is part. Picasso's easel has mirrored these currents and eddies to an almost transparent degree. Thus, while his canvases became places of torture as Europe's last pre-war summer drew to full height, he still paused in wonderment before a handful of glowing feathers, all that remained of a jaunty little bird his chauffeur had found dead in the street. Then, using only his brush, he gave it new wings . . . and restored it to life.

9. 4. 1939 $5\,^1/_2 \times 8\,^5/_8$

3. 6. 1939

$31\,^{7}/_{8} \times 21\,^{1}/_{4}$

For many Europeans the sorrows brought upon them by Hitler's Germany started September 1st, 1939, when his panzers and Stukas blitzed Poland. For most Spaniards chaos had struck two years earlier. For Picasso, being both Spanish and an adopted Frenchman living in Paris, which soon was to capitulate, the atmosphere of tragedy had been unending. He fought back the only way he could. Using his easel as artillery he fired barrages of paint and canvas which were almost as lethal as the heaviest shells, for when they burst over the heads of the enemy the concussion was felt in many lands. His mural *Guernica*, probably art's most damaging blockbuster, was reproduced by the multiple millions—on postcards, placards and posters, and in countless pamphlets and books—all of them stigmatizing the Falangistas and Nazis for that latter day massacre of innocents. Two more canvases, painted in April, 1939, spotlighted a full-bellied tomcat with bristling whiskers, glazed stare and bared teeth—from which dangled a nearly disembowled bird. Lunatic eyes caged the viewer. There was no escape. The cat, of course, was Adolf Hitler. Each one of us was the bird.

Although totally unrecorded until now, on June 3, 1939, Picasso began a series of chilling portraits in which the progressive destruction of everything dear was told in the face of his model. She was gowned in the sombre greys and black of a mourning duchess of Spain. For Picasso, the wake for the world had already started even though World War II had not yet begun.

3. 6. 1939

31 $^7/_8$ × 21 $^1/_4$

9. 6. 1939

24 × 15

168

When Picasso added this gaudy portrait to others of the same week it seemed as though his earlier, despairing mood had lifted, that he had returned to his sunny, carefree palette of the preceding year— then he painted hair-trigger madness in the eyes of this girl with a blood red birthmark on her throat. Later that day, in a second canvas, her eyes had narrowed to feline, icy slits through which she unblinkingly followed the viewer. Picasso had also painted another pair of same-day portraits at the beginning of the week in which her luxurious cascades of shoulder-length hair resembled roaring columns of smoke and fire. Of course, not one of these pictures was actually a portrait but his prophesy of a ruined world.

9. 6. 1939

24 × 15

17. 6. 1939

36 $^1/_4$ × 28

172

Dressed in flamboyant colors and a fantastic new hat, showered by tinseled starburst from a festival sky—no one would have guessed, seeing this painting alone, it was meant as a chapter marker in the history book of nations whose leaders' ambition was to conquer the earth. Yet, after matching the canvas to the other painted the same day, the portrait can only be read Picasso's way.

With the sea in the background of her vacation land, Picasso's heroine finally turned to the frantic little bird that had perched on her shoulder, shrilly singing there before flying away. But the song was wasted for the girl refused to listen nor did she look into her mirror where she would have seen not a bright summer poppy on her jaunty new hat, but a rising sun on a prowling dreadnought from Imperial Japan.

Forgetting sailboat and daisy and her picnic dreams, a forlorn little girl who had lost her way stood trapped in a field where flames reached the sky—her arms outstretched as though on a cross . . . crowned in a wreath that might have been thorns—spring's gentle promise martyred as a child who had strayed among men not playing that day.

18. 6. 1939

$^1/_4 \times 28\ ^3/_4$

23. 6. 1

24 × 1

178

At last it seemed as though no canvas could fully contain the desolation Picasso saw ahead; of a world—her face nearly destroyed—so stunned by the shell bursts which had left her scarred that her stare sought nothing. It was useless hiding and too late to run. Nine weeks later, World War II had begun.

Few subjects of the post-war years have excited Picasso's attention more than his own youngest child, Paloma. Portraits of her appeared on his easel almost from the day she was born. Progressively thereafter, as she lay asleep in her crib, learned to walk, then to eat with knife and fork and to ride her tricycle, and to draw faces beside her brother, Claude, Picasso concentrated all of his sensitivities upon portraying each new horizon seen in her unfolding life until it seemed that no barrier separated her world and his—that no years kept them apart. One of the most beautiful of these pictures was painted when Paloma was three, as she began poking inquisitive fingers into each toy that had been discovered two days earlier beneath the Christmas tree.

27. 12. 1953

51 $^1/_8$ × 38 $^1/_8$

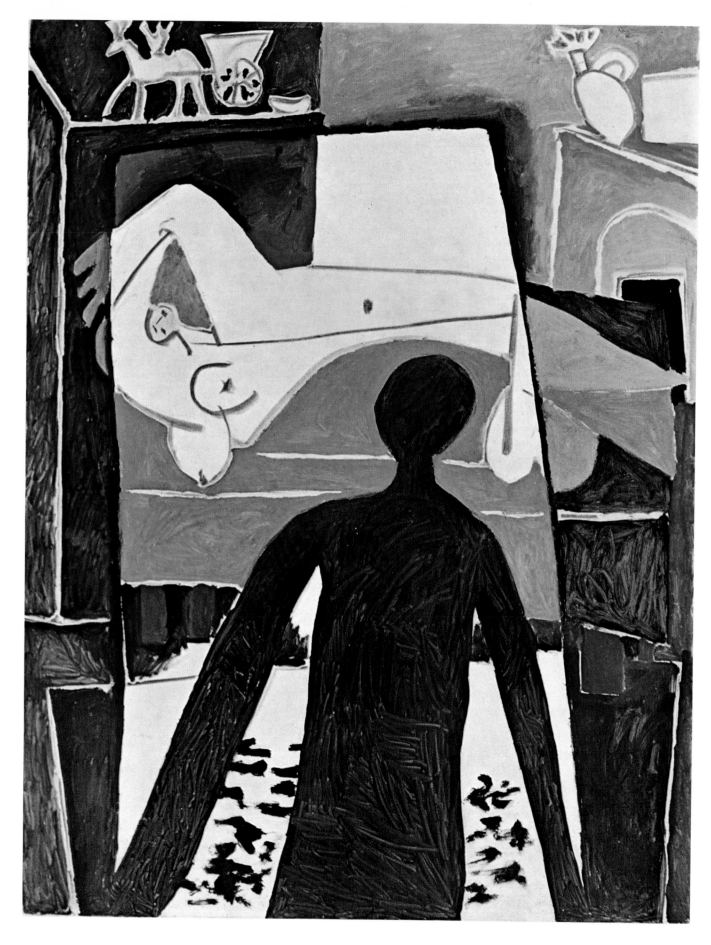

29. 12. 1953

51 $^1/_8$ × 38 $^1/_8$

The Maestro was standing beside me the day this painting was upon my easel to be photographed, so I had the opportunity of telling him that it was just about the strangest, most confusing composition I had run against in *La Californie*. He just shrugged—and I burst out laughing, accusing him of forgetting what it really meant. The day before, when seeing some of my transparencies projected, he had accused *me* of painting a canvas he claimed he never did. But now, the joke was over: he spun around, stepped to my easel and with a fencing finger almost poked holes in the canvas. " It was our bedroom. See my shadow? I'd just turned from the window—*now* do you see my shadow and the sunlight falling onto the bed and across the floor? See the toy cart on the dresser, and the little vase over the fireplace? They're from Sicily and still around the house. " As soon as he had provided the pass-key I knew exactly where it was. The black and white rug is still spread across the bedroom floor.

Hanging precariously on an old nail driven high into one of *La Californie*'s second floor sitting room walls, a portrait of Jacqueline Picasso reigns supreme. The room is her domain, complementing Picasso's studio as the other half of the great villa's heart. Painted in oil with charcoal, the picture has been at her side since shortly after she and the Maestro met. Much as she loves it and wants it nearby, she knows the enormity of the risk in keeping it in sight. Picasso may see the untouched canvas around her head as a challenge—and joyously set to work painting it one night.

5.10.54. pour ma chère Jacqueline
Picasso

10. 1954

4 × 28 3/4

12. 10. 1955

$27 \times 21\,^3/_4$

Cramped into a crowded corner of Jacqueline's sitting room in *La Californie*, between a circus distorting mirror and the doorway, there is—for me, at least—the most penetratingly revealing portrait Picasso has ever made of his wife. It is painted in greys and blacks. The bottom of the picture is practically bare canvas and the colors appear to have been applied almost indifferently, yet one immediately knows Jacqueline and the selfless soul who lies behind her eyes. By its very simplicity—as in the fullness of one heartbeat—it is complete. It is Jacqueline, the person who has offered to Picasso life's greatest gift and in so doing has shared his own incredible gift with us all.

Possibly—just possibly—this lone detail of a single Picasso, which looks straight into Jacqueline Picasso's eyes, perhaps this fragment of one portrait hints of the mystery still locked within all of the other Picassos in *La Californie*—and reveals something of what it must mean to Pablo Picasso to be an artist.

189

24. 6. 1958   18 $^1/_8$ × 21 $^5/_8$

Surprisingly, for an artist who has painted many of his pictures at night—whose real workday generally starts when most people in the nearby towns and countryside are asleep—Picasso confided once to me
that a subject which has proven extraordinarily elusive throughout his life, taunting him to be captured
on canvas, was Night herself.

In the summer of 1958, several months after finishing his mammoth series of prismatic canvases
inspired by Velasquez' *Las Meninas*, Picasso turned to portray his own dining room in *La Californie* with its
table that often serves as his workbench, the soaring windows, and Lump, his dachshund, curled asleep on the

190

8. 7. 1958   18 $\frac{1}{8}$ × 21 $\frac{5}{8}$

scarlet matador's cape covering the Maestro's favorite but disintegrating, over-stuffed chair. Although lamp-light cut the gloom, the interior of the villa was dominated by the stars and the moon, and by the ocean of the night outside the room. The picture was painted from memory in the villa's attic—under the glare of an unshaded 500-watt bulb—the same as when he painted a cake frosting landscape after we had driven with Jacqueline on a long-awaited vacation—of one day—to visit the Roman ruins at Les Baux, which are hidden among the grotesque limestone cliffs of Provence. Later, back in *La Californie*, the light in Picasso's third floor studio blazed through most of the night.

Perro, the Dalmatian, came to *La Californie* as a handful of spots at about the same time that Picasso and Jacqueline acquired the monumental *Château de Vauvenargues*, near Aix-en-Provence, and began scouting the local second-hand shops for equally massive furniture with which to furnish its ancient halls. As Perro grew to gangling, gentle doghood he developed a crush on Picasso which rivalled in scale both the château and its furnishings. He was simply head-in-the-clouds in love.

1959 II

× 51 1/8

18. 2. 1

39 ³/₈ ×

194

Jutting up through the treasury of portraits of Jacqueline stacked in Picasso's studio in *La Californie*, and others of Paloma and Claude, and still more paintings of those everyday subjects that surround him—the cavorting dogs, nesting pigeons, the view from his balcony—looming over them all is a series of gargantuan canvases painted during the last two years, in which Amazonian goddesses are depicted asleep, bathing, holding court, or just gazing out upon our twentieth century world as though it is a far stranger place than that from which they have come. In a few of these huge paintings there are clearly recognizable features of Jacqueline, but mostly they are of those people from the universe that Picasso invented.

2. 4. 1960

19 ⁵/₈ × 24

When Picasso stands painting in *La Californie* the doors of his top floor studio are generally thrown open, both to catch the night breeze from the Mediterranean just beyond his garden and so that he can visit with the pigeons who live on his balcony. They are friends. Many often wander into his room hoping to be fed from the sack of grain kept in the corner next to his colors. As he works, seeing the lights of Cannes go slowly out and the birds settle down for the night—knowing that Jacqueline is reading and waiting just below his brightly lit room—he fills the silence with his happiest song, simply that of brush upon canvas, while he paints alone.

196

12. 4. 1960

44 ⁷/₈ × 57 ¹/₂

Before photographing all of Picasso's Picassos in *La Californie* I experimented with the Maestro's most recent paintings since they were in his studio next to the room in which I worked. During the preliminary weeks of controlling lights and lenses, film, and even voltage in the villa, I necessarily reshot several canvases numerous times. Among them was this curiously contorted girl on the beach. One afternoon, the Maestro came to my room while she was perched again on my easel facing the lights. By then she was one of my favorites in the entire hoard, as I told Picasso. He shrugged—but then added, " In twenty-five years they may say that she is the best. "

197

During the many months that I worked in *La Californie*'s attic visits from Jacqueline were extremely rare, for her days were crowded with running the villa, shopping for the table, driving her daughter Kathy to school and trying to be constantly at Picasso's side through each waking hour. When he worked on the dinner table she sat quietly nearby. If he painted at his easel in the attic she sometimes sat there in his sagging old chair, or, if she felt that he wished to be completely alone, she stretched out in her sitting room just below his studio where she could hear him moving the easel, dragging canvases across the floor, or stamping around chasing visiting pigeons back to their perches outside his door. Thus, the day she and Janot, the chauffeur, called from beyond my blacked-out room I had no idea what could have brought them to the top of the villa.

Janot gingerly held something heavy bundled in an old newspaper while Jacqueline, in her excitement, almost danced around the room. Then the paper burst open and three fat eels wriggled for the floor. Jacqueline was still practically choking with laughter as she told of Picasso's reaction when they had shown him the eels as he lay shaving in bed.

Lunch was in the kitchen that day, with Jacqueline as chef. The three eels were guests of honor on a center plate of their own, served as an aromatic Mediterranean *matelote* in which no herb had been spared—a considerable achievement for someone who had not cooked often in her life. Later, when Picasso and I were both back at work, I heard Jacqueline call from the studio next door. She and the Maestro stood hand-in-hand looking at his easel where a still life had just appeared: three eels, a newspaper, a spicy onion, Jacqueline's purse which had bought them for the house and the knife that had prepared them for their trip to the table. After a few minutes, saying that he still was not finished, Picasso raised his brush and chased us out.

Half an hour later I heard Jacqueline once more on the stairs. This time her cry brought me running. Again they were holding hands, with pigeons swirling underfoot. On his easel glistened the new-born painting, its dedication scrawled so boldly it could be read from anywhere in the room. Together we carried it from his easel to mine to be photographed as a child in that first happy hour of life.

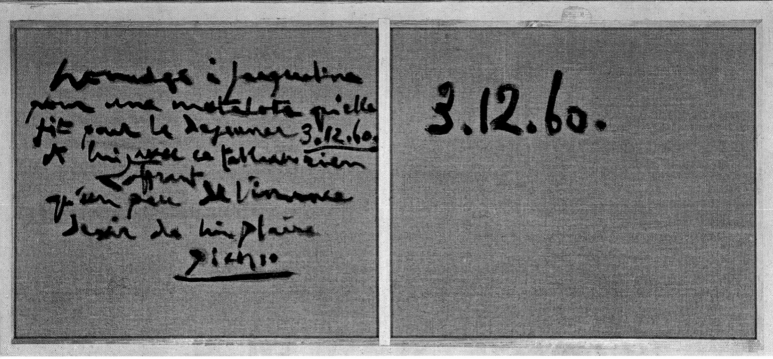

$19\,^{1}/_{2} \times 42\,^{1}/_{2}$

Homage to Jacqueline for a matelote that she prepared
for lunch 3. 12. 60 offering to her through this painting
a small portion of the immense desire I have to please her.
Picasso

PICASSO'S PICASSOS

Catalogue

1895-1960

VILLA LA CALIFORNIE

Size: Vertical dimension, first; horizontal dimension, second. Centimeters, left; inches, right.

Date: European system; day, month, year. If no day, then only the month and year are given; for example –.10.1957. When Picasso paints more than one canvas in a single day, he adds a Roman numeral after the date to place the picture in precise chronological sequence; for example: 12.10.1957.IV. Picasso began dating his work by day, month and year starting around 1923. Prior to 1923 most of his work was completely undated. Picasso has seen and checked this entire catalogue, and he himself attributed the dates given for all of his earlier pictures which are undated on the canvases.

Practically all of the paintings in *La Californie* are unsigned, as is Picasso's custom until offering a picture to his dealer for sale. The reason for several pictures remaining in Picasso's possession after being signed is known only to himself.

✱ : An asterisk designates each painting which is reproduced in the preceding color section.

Note: Several of the color plates reveal curious, dark lines, or spots, on various areas of the canvases. These are coatings of dust which have accumulated during the years of being stacked, unmoved, in Picasso's storage vaults. By the Maestro's own request, all of his paintings in *La Californie* were photographed exactly as I found them.

50   1895   29 $^1/_4$ × 19 $^1/_2$ 13 × 13   1895   5 $^1/_4$ × 5 $^1/_4$ 50 × 36   1895   19 $^3/_4$ × 14 $^1/_4$

23   1895/96   7 $^1/_4$ × 9 $^1/_8$ 60 × 71   1895/96   23 $^3/_4$ × 28   22 × 33   –. 4. 1896   8 $^7/_8$ × 13

× 14   1897/98   7 $^1/_4$ × 5 $^1/_2$ 46 × 55   1899   18 $^1/_8$ × 21 $^5/_8$ 150 × 100   1899   59 × 39 $^1/_2$

81 × 60   *1901*   32 × 23 ³/₄   17 × 15,5   *1901*   6 ⁵/₈ × 6 ¹/₈   23 × 16,5   *1901*   9 ¹/₈ ×

37 × 27   *1904*   14 ⁵/₈ × 10 ⁵/₈   34 × 25   *–. 8. 1904*   13 ³/₈ × 10   45 × 37   *1905*   17 ³/₄ ×

27 × 19   *1907*   10 ³/₄ × 7 ¹/₂   26 × 17   *1907*   10 ¹/₈ × 6 ⁵/₈   *   18 × 15   *1907*   7

× 14   1907/08   7 × 5 ⁵/₈   15,5 × 18   1907/08   6 ¹/₈ × 7   17,5 × 14   1907/08   6 ⁷/₈ × 5 ⁵/₈

81   1908   25 ⁵/₈ × 31 ⁷/₈   27 × 21   1908   10 ⁵/₈ × 8 ³/₈   21 × 27   1908   8 ³/₈ × 10 ⁵/₈

21   1908   10 ⁵/₈ × 8 ³/₈   21 × 27   1908   8 ³/₈ × 10 ⁵/₈   27 × 21   1908   10 ⁵/₈ × 8 ³/₈

27 × 21   1908 $10\,^5/_8 \times 8\,^3/_8$ 27 × 21   1908/09 $10\,^5/_8 \times 8\,^3/_8$ 27 × 21   1908/09 $10\,^5/_8 \times$

27 × 21   1908/09 $10\,^5/_8 \times 8\,^3/_8$ 27 × 21   1908/09 $10\,^5/_8 \times 8\,^3/_8$ 27 × 21   1908/09 $10\,^5/_8 \times$

27 × 21   1909 $10\,^5/_8 \times 8\,^3/_8$ 37 × 49   1912 $14\,^1/_2 \times 19\,^1/_4$ 38 × 38   1912 $14\,^7/_8 \times 1$

× 35   *9. 11. 1912* $10\,^5/_8 \times 13\,^3/_4$ $16 \times 11{,}5$ *1913/14* $6\,^3/_8 \times 4\,^1/_2$ 16×13 *1913/14* $6\,^1/_4 \times 5$

× 18   *1913/14* $4\,^7/_8 \times 7$ 38×50 *1913/14* $15 \times 19\,^3/_4$ 13×17 *1913/14* $5 \times 6\,^5/_8$

× 22   *1914* $6\,^1/_4 \times 8\,^5/_8$ 18×13 *1914* $7 \times 5\,^1/_4$ 11×14 *1914* $4\,^1/_4 \times 5\,^5/_8$

15 × 18   *1914*   6 × 7

23,5 × 11   *1914*   9 $^1/_4$ × 4 $^1/_4$

24 × 19   *1914*   9 $^1/_2$ ×

49 × 43   *1914*   19 $^1/_4$ × 16 $^7/_8$

82,5 × 119   *1918*   32 $^1/_2$ × 46 $^3/_4$ *

130 × 89   *1919*   51 $^1/$

81 × 100   *1919*   31 $^7/_8$ × 39 $^3/_8$

52 × 70   *1920*   20 $^1/_2$ × 27 $^1/_2$

33 × 41   *1922*   12 $^7/_8$ ×

22   1922 $5\,^1/_2 \times 8\,^5/_8$ 18×23 1922 7×9 72×60 1923 $28\,^1/_2 \times 23\,^1/_2$

$\times\ 173$ 1923 80×68 19×27 –. 5. 1923 $7\,^1/_2 \times 10\,^5/_8$ 130×97 –. 5. 1923 $51\,^1/_8 \times 38\,^1/_8$

24   7. 11. 1923 $13 \times 9\,^1/_2$ 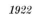 33×24 10. 11. 1923 $13 \times 9\,^1/_2$ 130×97 1924 $51\,^1/_8 \times 38\,^1/_8$

209

33 × 24   *1924*   *13 × 9 1/2*   *130 × 97*   *1925*   *51 1/8 × 38 1/8*   *200 × 150*   *1925*   *78 7/8 ×*

216,5 × 143,5   *1925* *85 1/4 × 56 1/2*   *14 × 24*   *1925*   *5 1/2 × 9 1/2*   *12 × 22*   *1925*   *4 3/4 ×*

35 × 27   *1925*   *13 3/4 × 10 5/8*   *24 × 16   9. 2. 1925   9 1/2 × 6 1/4*   *130 × 97*   *1926*   *51 1/8 ×*

210

× 256,5   1926   68   × 101   97 × 130   1926   38 $^1/_8$ × 51 $^1/_8$ 24 × 16   20. 11. 1926   9 $^1/_2$ × 6 $^1/_4$

16   25. 11. 1926   8 $^5/_8$ × 6 $^1/_4$ 22 × 14 –. 12. 1926   8 $^5/_8$ × 5 $^1/_2$ 22 × 14 –. 12. 1926   8 $^5/_8$ × 5 $^1/_2$

16   1. 12. 1926   8 $^5/_8$ × 6 $^1/_4$ 73 × 92   1927   28 $^3/_4$ × 36 $^1/_4$ 130 × 97   1927   51 $^1/_8$ × 38 $^1/_8$

55 × 55   *1928*   *21 ⁵/₈ × 21 ⁵/₈*   *162 × 130*   *–. 4. 1928*   *63 ³/₄ × 51 ¹/₈*   *33 × 22*   *9. 8. 1928*   *13 ×*

24 × 16   *9. 8. 1928 I*   *9 ¹/₂ × 6 ¹/₄*   *41 × 22*   *10. 8. 1928*   *16 ¹/₄ × 8 ⁵/₈*   *22 × 41*   *12. 8. 1928*   *8 ⁵/₈ ×*

24 × 35   *15. 8. 1928*   *9 ¹/₂ × 13 ³/₄*   *24 × 35*   *15. 8. 1928*   *9 ¹/₂ × 13 ³/₄*   *22 × 41*   *20. 8. 1928*   *8 ⁵/₈ × 1*

× 16   23. 8. 1928 $8\,^5/_8 \times 6\,^1/_4$ 195×130 1929 $76\,^3/_4 \times 51\,^1/_8$ 16×24 –. 2. 1929 $6\,^1/_4 \times 9\,^1/_2$

× 24   3. 4. 1929 $6\,^1/_4 \times 9\,^1/_2$ 195×130 5. 5. 1929 $76\,^3/_4 \times 51\,^1/_8$ 16×22 18. 8. 1929 $6\,^1/_4 \times 8\,^5/_8$

× 22   18. 8. 1929 $6\,^1/_4 \times 8\,^5/_8$ 16×22 23. 8. 1929 $6\,^1/_4 \times 8\,^5/_8$ * 14×24 24. 8. 1929 $5\,^1/_2 \times 9\,^1/_2$

22 × 14   24.8.1929   8 ⁵/₈ × 5 ¹/₂   22 × 14   25.8.1929   8 ⁵/₈ × 5 ¹/₂   22 × 14   1.9.1929   8 ⁵/₈ ×

130 × 162   –.11.1929   51 ¹/₈ × 63 ³/₄   50 × 66   1930   19 ³/₄ × 25 ³/₄   162 × 130   18.1.1930   63 ³/₄ × 5

14 × 22   11.1.1931   5 ¹/₂ × 8 ⁵/₈   46 × 61   4.2.1931   18 ¹/₈ × 24   195 × 130   11.3.1931   76 ³/₄ ×

214

× 195   8. 3. 1931   51 $^1/_8$ × 76 $^3/_4$ 130 × 97   1932   51 $^1/_8$ × 38 $^1/_8$ 33 × 24   9. 1. 1932   13 × 9 $^1/_2$

× 97   3. 3. 1932   51 $^1/_8$ × 38 $^1/_8$ 46 × 46   16. 5. 1932   18 $^1/_8$ × 18 $^1/_8$ 27 × 35   5. 2. 1933   10 $^5/_8$ × 13 $^3/_4$

24   10. 4. 1933   7 $^1/_2$ × 9 $^1/_2$ 97 × 130   25. 1. 1934   38 $^1/_8$ × 51 $^1/_8$ 22 × 35   9. 5. 1934   8 $^5/_8$ × 13 $^3/_4$

215

55 × 46   9. 3. 1935   21 ⁵/₈ × 18 ¹/₈   61 × 50   1936   24 × 19 ⁵/₈   55 × 46   2. 4. 1936   21 ⁵/₈ × 1

55 × 46   3. 4. 1936   21 ⁵/₈ × 18 ¹/₈   46 × 38   4. 4. 1936   18 ¹/₈ × 15   46 × 38   5. 4. 1936   18 ¹/₈ ×

46 × 55   6. 4. 1936   18 ¹/₈ × 21 ⁵/₈   55 × 46   9. 4. 1936   21 ⁵/₈ × 18 ¹/₈   61 × 50   11. 4. 1936   24 ×

216

× 46   13. 4. 1936 $21\,^5/_8 \times 18\,^1/_8$ * 55×46 13. 4. 1936 $21\,^5/_8 \times 18\,^1/_8$ * 61×50 15. 4. 1936 $24 \times 19\,^5/_8$ *

× 60   16. 4. 1936 $28\,^3/_4 \times 23\,^5/_8$ * 73×60 17. 4. 1936 $28\,^3/_4 \times 23\,^5/_8$ * 41×33 20. 4. 1936 $16\,^1/_8 \times 13$ *

× 38   22. 4. 1936 $18\,^1/_8 \times 15$ * 65×54 24. 4. 1936 $25\,^5/_8 \times 21\,^1/_4$ * 54×65 25. 4. 1936 $21\,^1/_4 \times 25\,^5/_8$ *

217

46 × 38   25. 4. 1936   18 $^1/_8$ × 15 ✱   73 × 60   26. 4. 1936   28 $^3/_4$ × 23 $^5/_8$ ✱   65 × 54   29. 4. 1936   25 $^5/_8$ × 2

65 × 54   30. 4. 1936   25 $^5/_8$ × 21 $^1/_4$ ✱   61 × 50   1. 5. 1936   24 × 19 $^5/_8$ ✱   61 × 50   1. 5. 1936   24 × 1

61 × 50   2. 5. 1936   24 × 19 $^5/_8$ ✱   73 × 60   −. 5. 1936   28 $^3/_4$ × 23 $^5/_8$ 65 × 54   −. 5. 1936   25 $^5/_8$ × 2

61   8. 12. 1936 $18\,^1/_8 \times 24$ 33×46 14. 12. 1936 $13 \times 18\,^1/_8$ 46×38 19. 12. 1936 $18\,^1/_8 \times 15$

41   22. 12. 1936 I $10\,^5/_8 \times 16\,^1/_8$ 27×35 22. 12. 1936 II $10\,^5/_8 \times 13\,^3/_4$ 97×130 29. 12. 1936 $38\,^1/_8 \times 51\,^1/_8$

65   1937 $36\,^1/_4 \times 25\,^5/_8$ 92×65 1937 $36\,^1/_4 \times 25\,^1/_2$ 100×81 5. 1. 1937 $39\,^3/_8 \times 31\,^7/_8$

100×81 6. 1. 1937 $39\,^3/_8 \times 31\,^7/_8$ 27×22 8. 1. 1937 $10\,^3/_4 \times 8\,^3/_4$ 46×61 8. 1. 1937 $18\,^1/_8$

38×46 15. 1. 1937 II $15 \times 18\,^1/_8$ 55×46 15. 1. 1937 III $21\,^5/_8 \times 18\,^1/_8$ 55×46 15. 1. 1937 IV $21\,^5/_8 \times$

33×41 16. 1. 1937 II $13 \times 16\,^1/_8$ 41×33 21. 1. 1937 $16\,^1/_8 \times 13$ 50×61 22. 1. 1937 $19\,^5/_8$

220

× 33   −. 2. 1937   16 $^1/_8$ × 13   50 × 65   −. 2. 1937   19 $^5/_8$ × 25 $^5/_8$ *   73 × 60   3. 2. 1937   28 $^3/_4$ × 23 $^5/_8$ *

× 60   3. 2. 1937   28 $^3/_4$ × 23 $^5/_8$ *   92 × 65   4. 2. 1937   36 $^1/_4$ × 25 $^5/_8$ *   61 × 46   6. 2. 1937   24 × 18 $^1/_8$

× 97   18. 2. 1937   51 $^1/_8$ × 38 $^1/_8$ 130 × 97   29. 2. 1937   51 $^1/_8$ × 38 $^1/_8$ 46 × 55   4. 3. 1937   18 $^1/_8$ × 21 $^5/_8$

73 × 60   6. 3. 1937   28 ³/₄ × 23 ⁵/₈

73 × 60   6. 3. 1937   28 ³/₄ × 23 ⁵/₈

61 × 50   6. 3. 1937   24 × 1⁹

61 × 50   6. 3. 1937   24 × 19 ⁵/₈

81 × 60   6. 3. 1937   31 ⁷/₈ × 23 ⁵/₈

130 × 97   11. 3. 1937   51 ¹/₈ × 3

19 × 24   18. 3. 1937   7 ¹/₂ × 9 ¹/₂

41 × 33   27. 3. 1937   16 ¹/₈ × 13

65 × 50   3. 4. 1937   25 ⁵/₈ × 1

46   21. 4. 1937   24 × 18 ¹/₈   22 × 16   30. 5. 1937   8 ⁵/₈ × 6 ¹/₄   16 × 22   18. 6. 1937   6 ¹/₄ × 8 ⁵/₈

22   19. 6. 1937   6 ¹/₄ × 8 ⁵/₈   16 × 22   19. 6. 1937   6 ¹/₄ × 8 ⁵/₈ *   46 × 33   24. 6. 1937   18 ¹/₈ × 13 *

38   9. 8. 1937   18 ¹/₈ × 15   130 × 97   9. 8. 1937   51 ¹/₈ × 38 ¹/₈   16 × 22   10. 8. 1937   6 ¹/₄ × 8 ⁵/₈ *

33 × 22   10. 8. 1937   13 × 8 ⁵/₈   55 × 46   14. 8. 1937   21 ⁵/₈ × 18 ¹/₈   55 × 46   15. 8. 1937   21 ⁵/₈ ×

61 × 50   28. 8. 1937   24 × 19 ⁵/₈   22 × 27   28. 8. 1937   8 ⁵/₈ × 10 ⁵/₈   61 × 50   29. 8. 1937 11   24 ×

81 × 65   2. 9. 1937 I   31 ⁷/₈ × 25 ⁵/₈   81 × 65   2. 9. 1937 II   31 ⁷/₈ × 25 ⁵/₈   81 × 65   4. 9. 1937 I   31 ⁷/₈ ×

65   4. 9. 1937 11   *31 ^{7}/$_8$ × 25 ^{5}/$_8$*   *27 × 35*   *–. 9. 1937*   *10 ^{5}/$_8$ × 13 ^{3}/$_4$*   *60 × 81*   *6. 9. 1937 11*   *23 ^{5}/$_8$ × 31 ^{7}/$_8$*

60   8. 9. 1937 11   *31 ^{7}/$_8$ × 23 ^{5}/$_8$*   *73 × 60*   *11. 9. 1937 I*   *28 ^{3}/$_4$ × 23 ^{5}/$_8$*   *55 × 46*   *1. 10. 1937*   *21 ^{5}/$_8$ × 18 ^{1}/$_8$*

46   18. 10. 1937   *21 ^{5}/$_8$ × 18 ^{1}/$_8$*   *55 × 46*   *18. 10. 1937*   *21 ^{5}/$_8$ × 18 ^{1}/$_8$*   *19 × 14*   *22. 10. 1937*   *7 ^{1}/$_2$ × 5 ^{1}/$_2$*

55 × 38   1. 11. 1937   21 ⁵/₈ × 15

55 × 38   20. 11. 1937   21 ⁵/₈ × 15

65 × 46   22. 11. 1937   25 ⁵/₈ ×

19 × 14   22. 11. 1937   7 ¹/₂ × 5 ¹/₂

55 × 46   23. 11. 1937   21 ⁵/₈ × 18 ¹/₈

46 × 38   3. 12. 1937   18 ¹/

19 × 10   3. 12. 1937   7 ¹/₂ × 4

61 × 50   4. 12. 1937   24 × 19 ⁵/₈

61 × 46   4. 12. 1937   24 ×

38   4. 12. 1937   21 $^5/_8$ × 15   46 × 38   4. 12. 1937   18 $^1/_8$ × 15 ✱   55 × 46   4. 12. 1937   21 $^5/_8$ × 18 $^1/_8$

38   4. 12. 1937   18 $^1/_8$ × 15   65 × 46   5. 12. 1937   25 $^5/_8$ × 18 $^1/_8$ 61 × 50   5. 12. 1937   24 × 19 $^5/_8$ ✱

× 46   8. 12. 1937   21 $^5/_8$ × 18 $^1/_8$ 35 × 27   10. 12. 1937   13 $^3/_4$ × 10 $^5/_8$ 22,5 × 16   18. 12. 1937   8 $^7/_8$ × 6 $^3/_8$

227

24 × 19   18. 12. 1937   9 ¹/₂ × 7 ¹/₂   *

35 × 24   19. 12. 1937   13 ³/₄ × 9 ¹/₂

55 × 46   1937/38   21 ⁵/₈ × 1

76 × 56,5   1937/38   30 × 22 ¹/₄   *

46 × 55   31. 12. 1937   18 ¹/₈ × 21 ⁵/₈   *

46 × 55   1. 1. 1938   18 ¹/₈ × 2

50 × 61   2. 1. 1938   19 ⁵/₈ × 24   *

46 × 55   7. 1. 1938   18 ¹/₈ × 21 ⁵/₈

50 × 61   7. 1. 1938   19 ⁵/₈ ×

228

46   7. 1. 1938   24 × 18 1/8

55 × 38   8. 1. 1938   21 5/8 × 15

81 × 60   8. 1. 1938   31 7/8 × 23 5/8

38   9. 1. 1938   18 1/8 × 15

46 × 38   9. 1. 1938   18 1/8 × 15   *

65 × 54   12. 1. 1938   25 5/8 × 21 1/4

38   14. 1. 1938   18 1/8 × 15

73 × 54   15. 1. 1938   28 3/4 × 21 1/4

46 × 38   15. 1. 1938   18 1/8 × 15

46 × 38   15. 1. 1938   18 $^1/_8$ × 15   73 × 60   16. 1. 1938   28 $^3/_4$ × 23 $^3/_4$ 65 × 54   22. 1. 1938   25 $^5/_8$ × 2

73 × 60   22. 1. 1938   28 $^3/_4$ × 23 $^5/_8$ 65 × 50   23. 1. 1938   25 $^5/_8$ × 19 $^5/_8$ 65 × 50   28. 1. 1938   25 $^5/_8$ ×

61 × 46   30. 1. 1938   24 × 18 $^1/_8$ *   19 × 27   30. 1. 1938   7 $^1/_2$ × 10 $^5/_8$ 73 × 60   4. 2. 1938   28 $^3/_4$ ×

× 54   *5. 2. 1938*   *28 ⁷/₈ × 21 ¹/₄*   *96 × 72*   *9. 2. 1938*   *37 ³/₄ × 28 ¹/₂*   *55 × 46*   *12. 2. 1938*   *21 ⁵/₈ × 18 ¹/₈*

$\times 54$ 5. 2. 1938 $28^{7}/_{8} \times 21^{1}/_{4}$ 96 × 72 9. 2. 1938 $37^{3}/_{4} \times 28^{1}/_{2}$ 55 × 46 12. 2. 1938 $21^{5}/_{8} \times 18^{1}/_{8}$

＊

$\times 24$ 18. 2. 1938 $7^{1}/_{2} \times 9^{1}/_{2}$ 19 × 24 19. 2. 1938 $7^{1}/_{2} \times 9^{1}/_{2}$ 19 × 24 26. 2. 1938 $7^{1}/_{2} \times 9^{1}/_{2}$

$\times 24$ 26. 2. 1938 $6^{1}/_{4} \times 9^{1}/_{2}$ 19 × 27 27. 2. 1938 $7^{1}/_{2} \times 10^{5}/_{8}$ 19 × 27 27. 2. 1938 $7^{1}/_{2} \times 10^{5}/_{8}$

19 × 24   6. 3. 1938   7 1/2 × 9 1/2 ★

46 × 38   14. 3. 1938   18 1/8 × 15

70 × 56   14. 3. 1938   27 1/2 ×

69 × 50   15. 3. 1938   27 1/4 × 19 1/2

62 × 49   16. 3. 1938   24 1/2 × 19 1/4

46 × 38   17. 3. 1938   18 1/8 ×

27 × 19   19. 3. 1938   10 5/8 × 7 1/2

57 × 43   22. 3. 1938   22 1/2 × 17

120 × 236   23. 3. 1938   47 3/8 ×

× 87   2. 4. 1938   48 ¹/₄ × 34 ¹/₄   143,5 × 119   4. 4. 1938   56 ¹/₂ × 46 ⁷/₈   100 × 81   6. 4. 1938   39 ³/₈ × 31 ⁷/₈

× 47   14. 4. 1938   25 ³/₈ × 18 ⁵/₈   61 × 46   16. 4. 1938   24 × 18 ¹/₈   81 × 72   26. 4. 1938   32 × 28 ¹/₄

29,5   –. 5. 1938   14 ⁷/₈ × 11 ⁵/₈   46 × 38   9. 5. 1938   18 ¹/₈ × 15   90 × 118   17. 5. 1938   35 ¹/₂ × 46 ⁵/₈

233

97 × 130   18. 5. 1938   38 ⅛ × 51 ⅛   44,5 × 41   20. 5. 1938   17 ½ × 16   38 × 29,5   22. 5. 1938   14 ⅞ ×

46 × 38   22. 5. 1938   18 ⅛ × 15   189 × 130   31. 5. 1938   74 ½ × 51   36 × 23   2. 6. 1938   14 ×

73 × 60   25. 6. 1938   28 ¾ × 23 ⅝   *   65 × 54   2. 7. 1938   25 ⅝ × 21 ¼   65 × 54   2. 7. 1938   25 ⅝ ×

234

54   *3. 7. 1938*   *25 ⁵/₈ × 21 ¹/₄*   *65 × 50*   *26. 7. 1938*   *25 ⁵/₈ × 19 ⁵/₈*   *61 × 46*   *27. 7. 1938*   *24 × 18 ¹/₈*

54   *28. 7. 1938*   *25 ⁵/₈ × 21 ¹/₄*   *61 × 50*   *6. 8. 1938*   *24 × 19 ⁵/₈*   *65 × 50*   *14. 8. 1938*   *25 ⁵/₈ × 19 ⁵/₈*

50   *14. 8. 1938*   *24 × 19 ⁵/₈*   *55 × 46*   *22. 8. 1938*   *21 ⁵/₈ × 18 ¹/₈*   *55 × 46*   *24. 8. 1938*   *21 ⁵/₈ × 18 ¹/₈*

235

55 × 46   28. 8. 1938   21 ⁵/₈ × 18 ¹/₈   65 × 50   30. 8. 1938   25 ⁵/₈ × 19 ⁵/₈   61 × 46   30. 8. 1938   24 ×

55 × 46   31. 8. 1938   21 ⁵/₈ × 18 ¹/₈   55 × 38   10. 9. 1938   21 ⁵/₈ × 15   92 × 73   29. 10. 1938   36 ¹/₄ ×

55 × 46   1. 11. 1938   21 ⁵/₈ × 18 ¹/₈   73 × 92   27. 11. 1938   28 ³/₄ × 36 ¹/₄   73 × 92   10. 12. 1938   28 ³/₄ ×

× 38   11. 12. 1938 $18\,^1/_8 \times 15$ 24×19 1938 $9\,^1/_2 \times 7\,^1/_2$ 61×50 31. 12. 1938 $24 \times 19\,^5/_8$

× 46   31. 12. 1938 $21\,^5/_8 \times 18\,^1/_8$ 73×60 1938/39 $28\,^3/_4 \times 23\,^5/_8$ 65×54 1. 1. 1939 $25\,^5/_8 \times 21\,^1/_4$

× 46   7. 1. 1939 $25\,^5/_8 \times 18\,^1/_8$ 92×73 8. 1. 1939 $36\,^1/_4 \times 28\,^3/_4$ 38×46 13. 1. 1939 $15 \times 18\,^1/_8$

237

100 × 81   21. 1. 1939   39 ³/₈ × 31 ⁷/₈ ✻   *19 × 24   22. 1. 1939   7 ¹/₂ × 9 ¹/₂*   *22 × 16   22. 1. 1939   8 ⁵/₈ ×*

24 × 19   22. 1. 1939   9 ¹/₂ × 7 ¹/₂   *22 × 16   22. 1. 1939   8 ⁵/₈ × 6 ¹/₄*   *19 × 14   12. 2. 1939   7 ¹/₂ ×*

19 × 14   12. 2. 1939   7 ¹/₂ × 5 ¹/₂   *14 × 19   12. 2. 1939   5 ¹/₂ × 7 ¹/₂*   *14 × 19   12. 2. 1939   5 ¹/₂ ×*

50   18. 2. 1939   24 × 19 ⁵/₈   19 × 14   22. 2. 1939   7 ¹/₂ × 5 ¹/₂   *   92 × 73   4. 3. 1939   36 ¹/₄ × 28 ³/₄

38   5. 3. 1939   21 ⁵/₈ × 15   55 × 38   5. 3. 1939   21 ⁵/₈ × 15   92 × 73   18. 3. 1939   36 ¹/₄ × 28 ³/₄

22   19. 3. 1939   10 ⁵/₈ × 8 ⁵/₈   27 × 22   19. 3. 1939   10 ⁵/₈ × 8 ⁵/₈   24 × 19   19. 3. 1939   9 ¹/₂ × 7 ¹/₂

19 × 24   19. 3. 1939   7 $^1/_2$ × 9 $^1/_2$ 24 × 16   19. 3. 1939   9 $^1/_2$ × 6 $^1/_4$ 61 × 46   29. 3. 1939   24 × 1

61 × 46   -. 3. 1939   24 × 18 $^1/_8$ 130 × 97   1. 4. 1939   51 $^1/_8$ × 38 $^1/_8$ 100 × 81   1. 4. 1939   39 $^3/_8$ × 3

27 × 22   2. 4. 1939   10 $^5/_8$ × 8 $^5/_8$ 14 × 22   9. 4. 1939   5 $^1/_2$ × 8 $^5/_8$ 41 × 24   9. 4. 1939   16 $^1/_8$ ×

240

100   22. 4. 1939   31 $^7/_8$ × 39 $^3/_8$ 65 × 54   21. 5. 1939   25 $^5/_8$ × 21 $^1/_4$ 65 × 54   21. 5. 1939   25 $^5/_8$ × 21 $^1/_4$

54 27. 5. 1939 31 $^7/_8$ × 21 $^1/_4$ 65 × 54   27. 5. 1939   25 $^5/_8$ × 21 $^1/_4$ *
81 × 54 3. 6. 1939 31 $^7/_8$ × 21 $^1/_4$

*
54 3. 6. 1939 31 $^7/_8$ × 21 $^1/_4$ 81 × 54 4. 6. 1939 31 $^7/_8$ × 21 $^1/_4$ 81 × 54 4. 6. 1939 31 $^7/_8$ × 21 $^1/_4$

61 × 38   *9. 6. 1939*   *24 × 15*   *61 × 38*   *9. 6. 1939*   *24 × 15*   *92 × 60* *10. 6. 1939* *36 ¹/₄ ×*

92 × 73   *17. 6. 1939*   *36 ¹/₄ × 28 ³/₄*   *92 × 73*   *17. 6. 1939*   *36 ¹/₄ × 28 ³/₄*   *61 × 38*   *18. 6. 1939*   *24*

92 × 73   *18. 6. 1939*   *36 ¹/₄ × 28 ³/₄*   *61 × 50*   *18. 6. 1939*   *24 × 19 ⁵/₈*   *61 × 50*   *23. 6. 1939*   *24 ×*

242

× 33   24. 6. 1939   18 ¹/₈ × 13   55 × 33   24. 6. 1939   21 ⁵/₈ × 13   162 × 130   6. 7. 1940   63 ³/₄ × 51 ¹/₈

× 130   15. 8. 1940   38 ¹/₈ × 51 ¹/₈   68 × 91,5   25. 6. 1943   26 ⁵/₈ × 36   79 × 60   17. 3. 1944   31 ¹/₈ × 23 ³/₄

× 60 7. 5. 1944 36 ¹/₄ × 23 ⁵/₈   73 × 116   15. 3. 1945   28 ³/₄ × 45 ⁵/₈   73 × 116   16. 3. 1945   28 ³/₄ × 45 ⁵/₈

175 × 250   1948   69 × 98 1/2

120,5×50   23.10.1948   47 1/2 × 19 5/8

100 × 81   5. 12. 1948 II   39 3/8 × 31

130 × 97   1950   51 1/8 × 38 1/8

116 × 89   1950   45 5/8 × 35

114 × 146   1951   44 7/8 × 57

60 × 72   1951   23 1/2 × 28 1/2

54 × 65   1951   21 1/4 × 25 1/2

55 × 46   8. 1. 1951   21 3/4 × 18

244

× 89   25. 1. 1951   45 $^5/_8$ × 35   130 × 97   3. 2. 1953   51 $^1/_8$ × 38 $^1/_8$ 100 × 81   21. 12. 1952   39 $^3/_8$ × 31 $^7/_8$
                                                                             3. 2. 1953

46   26. 2. 1953   24 × 18 $^1/_8$ 89 × 116   14. 12. 1953   35 × 45 $^5/_8$ 130 × 97   27. 12. 1953   51 $^1/_8$ × 38 $^1/_8$

× 97   29. 12. 1953   51 $^1/_8$ × 38 $^1/_8$ 81 × 65   12. 4. 1954   31 $^7/_8$ × 25 $^5/_8$ 81 × 65   15. 4. 1954   31 $^7/_8$ × 25 $^5/_8$

116 × 89   14. 5. 1954   45 5/8 × 35   *116 × 89   17. 5. 1954   45 5/8 × 35*   *116 × 89   3. 6. 1954   45 5/8 ×*

100 × 81   3. 6. 1954   39 3/8 × 31 7/8   *92 × 73   5. 10. 1954   36 1/4 × 28 3/4* *   146 × 114   8. 10. 1954   57 1/2 ×*

146 × 114   8. 10. 1954   57 1/2 × 44 7/8   *146 × 114   9. 10. 1954   57 1/2 × 44 7/8*   *92 × 73   11. 10. 1954   36 1/4 ×*

55 12. 10. 1955 27 × 21 ³/₄   80 × 190,5 15. 10. 1955 31 ¹/₂ × 75   190,5 × 80 22. 11. 1955 III 75 × 31 ¹/₂

65 29. 11. 1955 31 ⁷/₈ × 25 ⁵/₈   195 × 130 4. 1. 1956 76 ³/₄ × 51 ¹/₈   116 × 89 28. 3. 1956 45 ⁵/₈ × 35

146 30. 3. 1956 44 ⁷/₈ × 57 ¹/₂   195,5 × 259 29. 4. 1956 77 × 102   54 × 65 16. 9. 1956 21 ¹/₄ × 25 ⁵/₈

247

65 × 54   19. 6. 1957   25 ⁵/₈ × 21 ¹/₄   *146 × 114   27. 6. 1957   57 ¹/₂ × 44 ⁷/₈*   *194 × 260   17. 8. 1957   76 ¹/₂ × 1(...)*

46 × 38   20-26. 8. 1957   18 ¹/₈ × 15   *100 × 81   20. 8. 1957   39 ³/₈ × 31 ⁷/₈*   *100 × 81   21. 8. 1957   39 ³/₈ × 3(...)*

33 × 24   22. 8. 1957   13 × 9 ¹/₂   *41 × 33   26. 8. 1957   16 ¹/₈ × 13*   *41 × 33   27. 8. 1957   16 ¹/₈ ×(...)*

24   *27. 8. 1957*   *13 × 9 ¹/₂*   *33 × 24*   *27. 8. 1957*   *13 × 9 ¹/₂*   *19 × 14*   *28. 8. 1957*   *7 ¹/₂ × 5 ¹/₂*

14   *28. 8. 1957*   *7 ¹/₂ × 5 ¹/₂*   *46 × 38*   *4. 9. 1957*   *18 ¹/₈ × 15*   *35 × 27*   *4. 9. 1957*   *13 ³/₄ × 10 ⁵/₈*

× 27   *4. 9. 1957*   *13 ³/₄ × 10 ⁵/₈*   *35 × 27*   *5. 9. 1957*   *13 ³/₄ × 10 ⁵/₈*   *100 × 81*   *6. 9. 1957 11*   *39 ³/₈ × 31 ⁷/₈*

100 × 81   6. 9. 1957 III   39 3/8 × 31 7/8   *46 × 38   6. 9. 1957   18 1/8 × 15*   *41 × 33   6. 9. 1957   16 1/8*

100 × 81   7. 9. 1957 I   39 3/8 × 31 7/8   *33 × 24   7. 9. 1957 I   13 × 9 1/2*   *81 × 100   7. 9. 1957 II   31 7/8 ×*

130 × 97   11. 9. 1957   51 1/8 × 38 1/8   *100 × 81   12-14. 9. 1957   39 3/8 × 31 7/8*   *100 × 81   12. 9. 1957 II   39 3/8 ×*

114   12.9.1957 III   57 $^1/_2$ × 44 $^7/_8$

100 × 81   14. 9. 1957   39 $^3/_8$ × 31 $^7/_8$

130 × 162   15. 9. 1957   51 $^1/_8$ × 63 $^3/_4$

× 162   17. 9. 1957   51 $^1/_8$ × 63 $^3/_4$

33 × 41   17. 9. 1957   13 × 16 $^1/_8$

130 × 162   18. 9. 1957   51 $^1/_8$ × 63 $^3/_4$

× 130   19. 9. 1957   63 $^3/_4$ × 51 $^1/_8$

162 × 130   2. 10. 1957   63 $^3/_4$ × 51 $^1/_8$

130 × 162   3. 10. 1957   51 $^1/_8$ × 63 $^3/_4$

65 × 54   9. 10. 1957 I   25 ⁵/₈ × 21 ¹/₄   *65 × 54   9. 10. 1957 II   25 ⁵/₈ × 21 ¹/₄*   *92 × 73   10. 10. 1957 I   36 ¹/₄ ×*

73 × 55   10. 10. 1957 II   28 ³/₄ × 21 ³/₄   *116 × 89   10. 10. 1957 III   45 ⁵/₈ × 35*   *130 × 97   17. 10. 1957   51 ¹/₈ ×*

61 × 50   24. 10. 1957 I   24 × 19 ⁵/₈   *130 × 97   24. 10. 1957 II   51 ¹/₈ × 38 ¹/₈*   *130 × 97   24. 10. 1957 III   51 ¹/₈ ×*

252

× 97   24.10.1957 IV   51 $^{1}/_{8}$ × 38 $^{1}/_{8}$ 130 × 97   8.11.1957   51 $^{1}/_{8}$ × 38 $^{1}/_{8}$ 130 × 97   15.11.1957 I   51 $^{1}/_{8}$ × 38 $^{1}/_{8}$

× 97   15.11.1957 II   51 $^{1}/_{8}$ × 38 $^{1}/_{8}$ 35 × 27   17.11.1957 I   13 $^{3}/_{4}$ × 10 $^{5}/_{8}$ 24 × 19   17.11.1957 II   9 $^{1}/_{2}$ × 7 $^{1}/_{2}$

× 19   17.11.1957 III   9 $^{1}/_{2}$ × 7 $^{1}/_{2}$ 27 × 22   17.11.1957 IV   10 $^{5}/_{8}$ × 8 $^{5}/_{8}$ 24 × 19   17.11.1957 V   9 $^{1}/_{2}$ × 7 $^{1}/_{2}$

253

| 24 × 19 | 17. 11. 1957 VI | 9 $^1/_2$ × 7 $^1/_2$ | 14 × 19 | 2. 12. 1957 I | 5 $^1/_2$ × 7 $^1/_2$ | 14 × 19 | 2. 12. 1957 II | 5 $^1/_2$ × 7 |

| 16 × 22 | 2. 12. 1957 III | 6 $^1/_4$ × 8 $^5/_8$ | 116 × 89 | 3. 12. 1957 | 45 $^5/_8$ × 35 | 33 × 24 | 30. 12. 1957 | 13 × 9 |

| 199,5 × 201 | 13. 1. 1958 | 78 $^1/_2$ × 79 $^1/_4$ | 199,5 × 201 | 13. 1. 1958 | 78 $^1/_2$ × 79 $^1/_4$ | 195,5 × 259 | 18. 4. 1958 | 77 × |

× 97 28.4.1958 I $51^1/_8 \times 38^1/_8$ 130×97 28.4.1958 II $51^1/_8 \times 38^1/_8$ 146×114 29.4.1958 $57^1/_2 \times 44^7/_8$
                                                                                                        27-31. 5. 1958

× 63,5 29. 4. 1958 $33^1/_2 \times 25$ 100×81 ↑ 1-4. 5. 1958 $39^3/_8 \times 31^7/_8$ 162×130 28-31.5.1958 $63^3/_4 \times 51^1/_8$
                                                      100×81 ↓ 3-7. 5. 1958 $39^3/_8 \times 31^7/_8$ 7-9. 6. 1958

× 27 15.6.1958 II $13^3/_4 \times 10^5/_8$ 35×27 15.6.1958 III $13^3/_4 \times 10^5/_8$ $33 \times 24,5$ 15. 6. 1958 IV $13 \times 9^5/_8$

46 × 38   16. 6. 1958 II   18 ¹/₈ × 15   27,5 × 22   16. 6. 1958 III   10 ³/₄ × 8 ⁵/₈   55 × 38   17. 6. 1958   21 ⁵/₈

46 × 55   24. 6. 1958   18 ¹/₈ × 21 ⁵/₈ *   46 × 55   8. 7. 1958   18 ¹/₈ × 21 ⁵/₈ *   33 × 41   13. 7. 1958   13 × 1

27 × 35   26. 7. 1958   10 ⁵/₈ × 13 ³/₄   27 × 35   28. 7. 1958   10 ⁵/₈ × 13 ³/₄   61 × 46   8. 7.   24 × 1
                                                                                                 15. 8. 1958

195   19-27. 4. 1958   51 $^1/_8$ × 76 $^3/_4$ 100 × 81   8. 2. 1959   39 $^3/_8$ × 31 $^7/_8$ 130 × 97   13. 2. 1959 51 $^1/_8$ × 38 $^1/_8$
31. 5. 1958
1-7-9. 10. 1958

97 15. 2. 1959 51 $^1/_8$ × 38 $^1/_8$ 24 × 19   16. 2. 1959   9 $^1/_2$ × 7 $^1/_2$ 24 × 19   16. 2. 1959 III   9 $^1/_2$ × 7 $^1/_2$

16   16. 2. 1959 IV   8 $^5/_8$ × 6 $^1/_4$ 162 × 130   18. 2. 1959 II   63 $^3/_4$ × 51 $^1/_8$ 19 × 27   19. 2. 1959   7 $^1/_2$ × 10 $^5/_8$

146 × 114 1-18-19-22.2.1959 57 ¹/₂ × 44 ⁷/₈
8-9. 3. 1959

146 × 114   19. 3. 1959 I   57 ¹/₂ × 44 ⁷/₈

162 × 130   19.3.1959 II   63 ³/₄ ×

114 × 146   30. 1. 1960   44 ⁷/₈ × 57 ¹/₂

140 × 194,5   30. 1. 1960   55 × 76 ¹/₂

27 × 19   3. 2. 1960   10 ⁵/₈ ×

194,5 × 140   3. 2. 1960   76 ¹/₂ × 55

195,5 × 280,5   3. 2. 1960   77 × 110 ¹/₂

38 × 46   10. 2. 1960 I   15 ×

× 46   10. 2. 1960 11   15 × 18 ¹/₈   38 × 46   12. 2. 1960   15 × 18 ¹/₈   116 × 89   13. 2. 1960 I   45 ⁵/₈ × 35

27   13. 2. 1960 11   7 ¹/₂ × 10 ⁵/₈   35 × 27   13. 2. 1960 111   13 ³/₄ × 10 ⁵/₈   130 × 97   14. 2. 1960   51 ¹/₈ × 38 ¹/₈

× 114   14. 2. 1960   57 ¹/₂ × 44 ⁷/₈   100 × 81   18. 2. 1960   39 ³/₈ × 31 ⁷/₈   61 × 50   19. 2. 1960   24 × 19 ⁵/₈

259

55 × 46   19. 2. 1960   21 $^5/_8$ × 18 $^1/_8$ 55 × 46   19. 2. 1960   21 $^5/_8$ × 18 $^1/_8$ 50 × 61   21. 2. 1960   19 $^5/_8$

61 × 50   21. 2. 1960   24 × 19 $^5/_8$ 38 × 46   8. 3. 1960 IV   15 × 18 $^1/_8$ 65 × 54   10. 3. 1960 I   25 $^5/_8$ ×
            6. 3. 1960

81 × 65   10. 3. 1960 II   31 $^7/_8$ × 25 $^5/_8$ 130 × 97   1. 4. 1960   51 $^1/_8$ × 38 $^1/_8$ 50 × 61   2. 4. 1960   19 $^5/_8$

× 89   2. 4. 1960   45 $^5/_8$ × 35   100 × 81   2. 4. 1960   39 $^3/_8$ × 31 $^7/_8$ 92 × 73   3. 4. 1960   36 $^1/_4$ × 28 $^3/_4$
10. 5. 1960   10. 5. 1960

× 195   5. 4. 1960   51 $^1/_8$ × 76 $^3/_4$ 114 × 146   12. 4. 1960   44 $^7/_8$ × 57 $^1/_2$ 100 × 81   23. 4. 1960   39 $^3/_8$ × 31 $^7/_8$

× 46   2. 5. 1960 I   15 × 18 $^1/_8$ 54 × 65   2. 5. 1960 II   21 $^1/_4$ × 25 $^5/_8$ 54 × 65   2. 5. 1960 III   21 $^1/_4$ × 25 $^5/_8$

50 × 108   3. 12. 1960   19 $^1/_2$ × 42 $^1/_2$ *

Photographic Index

it to Pallarés as a memento of their visit. Instead of just signing the print Picasso sat down at th[e] dinner table and, in a few minutes, transformed my photograph into a Bacchanalian revelry wit[h] himself, bearded and wreathed in laurel, playing a major role—while shy Pallarés was transfigure[d] from a delicate octogenarian into a robust Roman senator holding the wine of a good life hig[h.] As with so many of his serious, early works in Cubism, where he included reality in the form [of] printed words, Picasso here left untouched the single most realistic object in the entire photograp[h:] the cigarette in his left hand.

PAGE 26: Picasso, as he sits thinking, is a man apart. He is so completely isolated from the local scene tha[t] I have never known nor heard of anyone who interrupted his sudden moods of unmoving, un[-] blinking, absolute silence—the silence that dominates a crowded room more completely than an[y] act, or word of conversation. To see Picasso thinking is simply an unforgettable experienc[e.]

PAGES 28-29: No single landmark is more renowned in modern art than Sainte-Victoire, the mountain tha[t] looms high above the town of Aix-en-Provence in southern France. For it was Sainte-Victoir[e] which served as Cézanne's model in his almost innumerable canvases where he sought solution[s] to the mysteries of light and shadow, as translated in colors. Cézanne painted the western an[d] southern sides of the mountain, including in most of his works the rocky pinnacle that crowns th[e] mass of lower cliffs and stone cascades. The northern slopes of Sainte-Victoire are dominated b[y] the ancient *Château de Vauvenargues*, which sits on a lower knoll of its own. Picasso bought th[e] citadel landmark in 1958 and, as the months passed, slowly moved a few simple furnishings int[o] its enormous halls. I saw it for the first time one afternoon in autumn. We had been heade[d] back to Cannes from Nîmes, where Picasso had journeyed to visit an obscure bullfighter who[m] he heard had been gored the week before. As we approached the château late afternoon sunligh[t] was slanting into the valley from across the hills. Picasso stood at my side while I photographe[d] the scene, explaining with a casual tilt of the head that all of the land climbing to the horizon[,] including the peak of Sainte-Victoire, had come with the château and now was his. I turne[d] from my camera to tell him how much the rolling land reminded me of the mountains of souther[n] Spain but he had already begun to speak with Jacqueline, worriedly making sure that a heav[y] sweater and a special envelope had been safely left for the destitute bullfighter lying wounde[d] in a strange land.

PAGES 30-31: A few minutes after Picasso and Jacqueline first showed me *Vauvenargues*, I looked over his head t[o] see the most remarkable combination of natural phenomenon with newsbreak timing it has eve[r] been my experience to enjoy. As he stood gazing out over the peak of Sainte-Victoire, dresse[d] in a Tyrolean hat and an aviator's quilted jacket, evening sunlight shot across the hills to spot[-] light him and his new home—creating a perfect rainbow, which enframed them both under its arc[.]

PAGES 32-33: During the scattered months of each year that Picasso and Jacqueline live in *Vauvenargues* ther[e] is practically no meeting between the owners of the massive château and the townspeople of th[e] nearby village of Vauvenargues. And yet, exactly as when he lives in semi-isolation in his vill[a] *La Californie*, Picasso displays an almost mystic degree of awareness of other lives as they orbi[t] around him and, somehow, maintains intimate contact with the outside world—its current news[,] latest books, most pressing crises—and the individuals who give it character. Newspapers, visitors[,] television (which he watches each night at eight when not actually painting, for half an hour o[r] general commentary telecast from Paris) certainly account for some of his information sources, yet profound authorities in specialized fields who have called as guests in his home leave perplexed and astonished by Picasso's possession of real knowledge in areas far afield from those associated with art. During my own several years of being near him, I have often been jolted by his revealing an almost photographic memory and that rarest of mental gifts, total recall. This pertains not only to things that we have done or spoken about together during these years, but also to events occuring throughout his life. The days that he spent as a guest in the apartment of Gertrude and Leo Stein in Paris, around the turn of the century, are as vivid as yesterday's activities to the Maestro. Although he speaks no English, he will often insert the precise English word into our conversation when he finds me searching for the exact Spanish word to make a point. One of the funniest of these incidents happened the day I was describing—unflatteringly—someone who had once visited *La Californie*. Picasso grinned in agreement, then added that the person would have made a marvelous " muse ". I simply couldn't get the connection, and told him so. In a flash his eyes turned tragic, his face sagged, while his hands—palms out—shot to his forehead. " Como un muse, Dooncan—un *muse*. " A moose! Of course, and he was so very right it was painful. Asking him where he had ever heard of a moose, he explained that " Jertrude " had shown him pictures and told him what they were called—once—around 1907.

PAGES 34-35: Shortly after acquiring the *Château de Vauvenargues* Picasso transformed its cavernous second floor salon into a studio by the simple process of moving in with his easel and starting to paint. Curiously, while watching him sitting almost motionless studying his most recent canvases, it seemed that I no longer was a guest of the Grand Master of modern art but was a visitor to the studio of Vermeer, or Peter de Hooch—to an Old Master of traditional art. Within a few months after taking this photograph I saw more than fifty paintings lining the walls around the studio, with others overflowing into nearby rooms, in vivid contrast to the classical grandeur of the Renaissance fireplace at the end of the ancient salon. Despite its colossal proportions the mantlepiece was completely dominated by the few brilliant paintings below.

PAGE 36: Of all the pictures painted in *Vauvenargues*, one of the most appealing is this of a boy dressed in the ragamuffin tatters of the homeless left in the wake of Napoleon's attack upon Spain at the beginning of the nineteenth century. It is a canvas that could have come only from the hand of a Spanish master, in the tradition of Velasquez or Goya, yet no one but Pablo Picasso ever could have actually painted it. The Maestro and Jacqueline view the little fellow as an individual, as a child born in *Vauvenargues*, for whom the great château is home. Jacqueline calls him " Tonto ", " The Little Fool ", but in an endearing way. Picasso, typically, has no name for him or the canvas. He simply greets him like a friend each time they meet. Actually, as far as I have been able to ascertain, Picasso has named only one canvas in his life: *Guernica*. Names apparently have no meaning for him. I remember the evening when he turned to his young son, Claude, asking him to bring something from his work table in the next room. Instead of " Claude ", Picasso called out " Octavio ", which brought first a look of bewilderment, then tears to Claude's eyes— then laughter, when Jacqueline and I made fun of the Maestro for his ability to remember everything *except* names. Several times I have seen him searching for even Jacqueline's name, while I, to Claude's delight, once ended up as " Ishmael ". For Picasso, names have no real significance. It is what we are and what we do that counts.

Painting Index

age	Materiels and technique	Dimensions	Date
25	Oil on canvas	$18\,^1/_8 \times 13$	24.6.1937
26	Oil on canvas	$24 \quad \times 19\,^5/_8$	29.8.1937
27	Oil on canvas	$6\,^1/_4 \times 8\,^5/_8$	10.8.1937
	(This painting was switched in the layout of the book with the painting on page 126, to improve the graphic balance of these two pages. I took this liberty with the otherwise chronological order of the layout of color plates because the two paintings appear on facing pages where the juxtaposition can easily be seen)		
28	Oil on canvas	$31\,^7/_8 \times 25\,^5/_8$	4.9.1937 I
29	Oil on canvas	$23\,^5/_8 \times 31\,^7/_8$	6.9.1937 II
30	Oil on canvas	$31\,^7/_8 \times 23\,^5/_8$	8.9.1937 II
31	Oil on canvas	$28\,^3/_4 \times 23\,^5/_8$	11.9.1937 I
33	Oil on canvas	$21\,^5/_8 \times 18\,^1/_8$	18.10.1937
35	Oil on canvas	$18\,^1/_8 \times 15$	4.12.1937
37	Oil on canvas	$24 \quad \times 19\,^5/_8$	5.12.1937
38	Gouache on panel	$9\,^1/_2 \times 7\,^1/_2$	18.12.1937
40	Collage of paper, gouache, on canvas	$30 \quad \times 22\,^1/_4$	1937-1938
41	Oil and charcoal on canvas	$18\,^1/_8 \times 21\,^5/_8$	31.12.1937
42	Oil and charcoal on canvas	$18\,^1/_8 \times 21\,^5/_8$	1.1.1938
43	Oil, pencil and charcoal on canvas	$19\,^5/_8 \times 24$	2.1.1938
45	Pastel and oil on canvas	$18\,^1/_8 \times 15$	9.1.1938
46	Oil on canvas	$25\,^5/_8 \times 21\,^1/_4$	22.1.1938
47	Oil on canvas	$24 \quad \times 18\,^1/_8$	30.1.1938
49	Oil on canvas	$21\,^5/_8 \times 18\,^1/_8$	12.2.1938
50	Oil on canvas	$7\,^1/_2 \times 9\,^1/_2$	6.3.1938
53	Oil on canvas	$28\,^3/_4 \times 23\,^5/_8$	25.6.1938
54	Pastel on canvas	$9\,^1/_2 \times 7\,^1/_2$	1938
55	Oil on canvas	$28\,^3/_4 \times 36\,^1/_4$	27.11.1938
56	Oil on canvas	$25\,^5/_8 \times 18\,^1/_8$	7.1.1939
57	Oil on canvas	$39\,^3/_8 \times 31\,^7/_8$	21.1.1939
58	Oil on canvas	$5\,^1/_2 \times 7\,^1/_2$	12.2.1939
59	Oil on canvas	$7\,^1/_2 \times 5\,^1/_2$	22.2.1939
61	Oil on canvas	$51\,^1/_8 \times 38\,^1/_8$	1.4.1939
63	Oil on canvas	$5\,^1/_2 \times 8\,^5/_8$	9.4.1939
64	Oil on canvas	$31\,^7/_8 \times 21\,^1/_4$	3.6.1939
67	Oil on canvas	$31\,^7/_8 \times 21\,^1/_4$	3.6.1939
68	Oil on canvas	$24 \quad \times 15$	9.6.1939
71	Oil on canvas	$24 \quad \times 15$	9.6.1939
72	Oil on canvas	$36\,^1/_4 \times 28\,^3/_4$	17.6.1939
75	Oil on canvas	$36\,^1/_4 \times 28\,^3/_4$	17.6.1939
77	Oil on canvas	$36\,^1/_4 \times 28\,^3/_4$	18.6.1939
78	Oil on canvas	$24 \quad \times 19\,^5/_8$	23.6.1939
81	Oil on canvas	$51\,^1/_8 \times 38\,^1/_8$	27.12.1953
82	Oil on canvas	$51\,^1/_8 \times 38\,^1/_8$	29.12.1953
85	Oil and charcoal on canvas	$36\,^1/_4 \times 28\,^3/_4$	5.10.1954
86	Oil and charcoal on canvas	$27 \quad \times 21\,^3/_4$	12.10.1955
89	Oil and charcoal on canvas	(detail of 186)	12.10.1955
90	Oil on canvas	$18\,^1/_8 \times 21\,^5/_8$	24.6.1958
91	Oil on canvas	$18\,^1/_8 \times 21\,^5/_8$	8.7.1958
93	Oil on canvas	$63\,^3/_4 \times 51\,^1/_8$	18.3.1959 II
94	Oil on canvas	$39\,^3/_8 \times 31\,^7/_8$	18.2.1960
96	Oil on canvas	$19\,^5/_8 \times 24$	2.4.1960
97	Oil on canvas	$44\,^7/_8 \times 57\,^1/_2$	12.4.1960
99	Oil on canvas	$19\,^1/_2 \times 42\,^1/_2$	3.12.1960

Now that *Picasso's Picassos* is almost finished it seems really quite incredible that it should exist at all and still be scheduled to appear this autumn on the Maestro's eightieth birthday, October 25th. This was the target publication date set when I originally embarked upon the project a year and a half ago, after Picasso first gave me permission to photograph his unknown paintings. At that time he was practically submerged in paint, canvas, ceramics and a massive folio of china ink drawings of picadors—in other words, tirelessly working, typically himself. Also typical—although I immediately assembled all of the equipment I thought I might need and moved temporarily to Cannes—another six months were to disappear before he was to turn one day and abruptly ask why I wasn't shooting the paintings! Within twelve hours he, Jacqueline and I had cleared a room on the villa's top floor next to his studio and I had moved in with all of my gear to start work. At that time no one, including Picasso himself, knew precisely how many paintings were stored in the villa. However, having actually seen several hundred canvases in one room, I came to an immediate decision about copying them. It was greeted with astonishment and almost total scepticism by my photographer friends who thought I was compounding the difficulties of the project into the realm of the nearly impossible, if I hoped to achieve quality reproductions. Even though unprecedented in the world of art books—where the 4×5 inch plate is considered a miniature—I had decided to shoot Picasso's Picassos with 35mm cameras.

My decision to copy Picasso's unknown paintings with 35mm was dictated by the sheer bulk of the hoard itself. I estimated there were more than five hundred paintings in *La Californie*. Even if I encountered no major obstacles in the project, I planned to shoot at least nine exposures of each painting: three exactly on exposure; three, half a stop under; three, half a stop over. That meant a minimum of 4500 shots would be needed to cover the treasure even under ideal conditions and without the slightest mistake anywhere along the line. I'd been a professional too long to expect *that*!

I had, of course, considered the project from the big camera point of view, recognizing the obvious merits of the huge transparency over the miniature. But, I also faced one insoluble question—where would I handle and process four thousand five hundred sheets of film? No private facilities in Europe were available or adequate for such a large scale operation. I would be shooting and shipping from a small town on the French Riviera. Many days, even weeks, would elapse between exposure and examination of transparencies—which meant that I would be in Picasso's attic forever. A marvelous fate but also somewhat unrealistic. He had plenty with which to occupy himself without having a photographer blowing the fuses in the entire villa—which I did several times—leaving the world's greatest artist at his easel, blacked out.

Instead of 4500 transparencies, the total was closer to 8000 before I finally finished photographing all of Picasso's Picassos in *La Californie*. One hundred canvases were reshot four times. The first was due to faulty film emulsion which gave everything an olive hue. The second shooting was tossed out after I saw a bluish tone permeating the greys (which I first had thought was caused by an unnoticed rise in the line voltage in the villa, but which actually was a temporary characteristic at one of the color laboratories where my work was being processed). The third was caused by my own carelessness: I reshot the hundred paintings still again after I discovered that my horizontal and vertical lines simply did not jibe with the borders of the transparency mounts. Somehow, despite all precautions—measurements from the floor to the center of lens and center of canvas, measurements to each corner of every painting from the center of the lens, use of a surveyor's bubble level on the painting and the easel and my camera for *every* setup—no two lines were parallel. The solution was as simple as the cause was stupid. I had overlooked the obvious. The films were being glued unevenly into the cardboard mounts right in the processing plant. Once removed from their mounts the parallels of each copied painting were absolutely true. By the time I discovered my own error I'd already reshot the same paintings for the fourth time.

After considerable trial and elimination of equipment, one basic setup was established in *La Californie's* attic. The room itself, which has a neutral grey ceiling, was draped with lusterless black cloth. During shooting all focusing and side lights were extinguished. Illumination was from six number 2 Photofloods mounted in vertical banks of three lights apiece on mobile stands. Special deep-cone but flat-light reflectors, two heavy-duty lightstands and an Ianiro three kilowatt transformer were brought from Rome where the equipment is made especially for the Italian movie industry. Color temperature was controlled by holding the illumination to within a two volt variation at the bulbs themselves.

Basic exposure for middle-scale paintings was two seconds at F 6.3 with the lights placed approximately 30 degrees off the surface plane of the canvases, 12-15 feet from the easel. Exposure was determined by the use of both Weston Master IV and Heiland Pentax Spot meters. Kodak color control patches, grey scale and register marks were placed at the central edges and corners of each painting. Every painting bore a card upon which were printed an identification number for the canvas, its size, and the date when it was painted. A gummed identification number was also affixed to the spreader of each canvas. To facilitate the shooting of paintings of identical sizes, control marks were made upon the floor so that the tripod could be moved and returned to its exact position without undue loss of time. There was no average time required for copying a painting. They ran from fifteen minutes, for the easy ones, to well over an hour for one of the collages where surface reflections made the task seemingly impossible, if I wished to obtain true color rendition of the painting. The film for the entire project was Type A Kodachrome which was processed in Paris and Lausanne by Kodak. Of course, all of the rolls of film were of the same emulsion number and the same expiration date.

The camera was a single lens Alpa 6 c Reflex, fitted with an apochromatic Kern Macro-Switar 50mm F 1.8 lens. Technicians at the Alpa factory replaced the conventional groundglass of the camera with one specially marked with control grids spaced one and a half millimeter apart. Supplementary lenses (for extremely large and very small canvases) were the 35mm Curtagon F 2.8, 75mm Xenar F 3.5 and 100mm Kinoptik F 2. Each of the supplementary lenses was fitted with an Alpa 40 filter to correct it to the color characteristics of the Kern Macro-Switar, unfiltered. All photographs of Picasso himself, in the introduction, were made with Leica M-3D cameras fitted with Canon 50mm F 1.2, or Canon 25mm F 3.5 lenses, on Daylight Kodachrome.

Today, only three months remain before all deadlines run out. Then the book must be ready for its birthday, together with the Maestro's. Four of Switzerland's finest engraving plants, two binderies and all of the presses at Imprimerie Centrale, in Lausanne, are operating full speed to complete the first edition which, for America alone, will fill twelve railway freight cars. At this point it looks as though *Picasso's Picassos* could only have been made with 35mm if we were to hit our deadline—and still fulfill everything latent in the Maestro's voice when he first agreed that I reveal his unknown paintings, " but, only in color! "

⁊sanne, 25, July 1961   D.D.D.

PRINTED IN SWITZERLAND